The Immigration Paradox

- including 15 Tips for Winning Immigration Cases

Attorney Charles Jerome Ware

WWW.CHARLESJEROMEWARE.COM
Former United States Immigration Judge

iUniverse, Inc.
New York   Bloomington

The Immigration Paradox
- including 15 Tips for Winning Immigration Cases

iUniverse books may be ordered through booksellers or by contacting:

iUniverse
1663 Liberty Drive
Bloomington, IN 47403
www.iuniverse.com
1-800-Authors (1-800-288-4677)

Because of the dynamic nature of the Internet, any Web addresses or links contained in this book may have changed since publication and may no longer be valid.

ISBN: 978-1-4401-7192-5 (sc)
ISBN: 978-1-4401-7193-2 (ebk)

Printed in the United States of America

iUniverse rev. date: 9/23/2009

Author's Note

An Immigration Paradox develops
when American immigration
policy is subjected to Government
benign neglect.

Charles Jerome Ware
Former U.S. Immigration Judge

— "The Bush Administration is tightening immigration now. In order to cross [the border] into the United States, you have to have legal documentation or a 95-mile-an-hour fast ball." [David Letterman, 2008]

— "Immigration is the big issue right now. Earlier today, the Senate voted to build a 370-mile fence along the Mexican border...Experts say a 370-mile fence is the perfect way to protect a border that is 1,900 miles long." [Conan O'Brien, 2008]

— "Proponents of the amnesty program for illegal (undocumented) immigrants say they are willing to take on jobs Americans are not willing to do. You know, like come up with an immigration policy." [Jay Leno, 2008]

Immigration, though subject to late-night comedic commentary, has always been a controversial, complex, and very important issue in American public policy. In fact, the historic and fundamental importance of immigration in American culture, in combination with the increasing controversy and complexities involving it, has created an immigration paradox.

In America, no human being is "illegal."

Immigration: the movement of persons into a foreign country for the purpose of permanently residing in that country (See, 128 F. 375, 380; Barron's Law Dictionary, 3rd Edition).

American immigration, or emigration to America, therefore, refers to the movement of nonresidents to the United States. It has been, and continues to be, a major source of population increase, economic growth, and diverse cultural changes throughout much of American history.

With the exception of the original native American Indians, all other Americans are either immigrants or descendants of immigrants. This influx of non-native Americans (immigrants) from many different cultures, societies, geographic areas, and languages has always presented challenges. The political, socioeconomic, and financial components of immigration in the United States have caused both controversy and strife concerning race and ethnicity, economic and financial empowerment, religion, and political alliances, among others.

According to the most recent census figures, there are over three hundred and two million people living in the United States. Conservative estimates place our nation's documented and undocumented (so-called "unauthorized") immigrant population at over forty million persons. That means about one in eight U.S. residents is foreign-born.

America is a nation of immigrants; yet, one of the most highly debated public policy issues discussed today is the so-called "immigration problem." According to the Center for Immigration studies in a November 2007 report, more than 10.3 million immigrants have arrived in the United States since the year 2000. This 2000 to 2007 period represents the highest seven-year timeline of immigration in American history. Further, the Center states that more than half (or about 5.6 million) of these foreign-born new arrivees are estimated to be undocumented.

Immigration, and in particular, undocumented or so-called illegal immigration, is a heated subject in modern-day politics.

As a former United States Immigration Judge, I have always been amazed by the lack of knowledge shown by our elected officials particularly, and the American public generally, over the issue of immigration. As a result, I believe, views on immigration tend to gravitate towards the extremes.

In a nation of immigrants, in which the land was taken from the natives by immigrants, the established immigrants either despise new immigrants to the extreme or adopt new immigrants to the extreme. This shortage of centrist immigration views over time has, again, contributed to the "immigration paradox" that I discuss in this book.

The history of immigration to America, the appropriately self-described "land of immigrants," is an interesting journey in American life. There have been multiple waves of immigrants coming to this country, from the British Pilgrims to the current-day Hispanics and other nationalities.

Even though the continuing influx of new immigrants from different cultures will undoubtedly present challenges, America has historically benefited in many ways from its immigrant populations and there is no reason to think that the United States will not continue to be energized by its new residents.

Though intertwined with some humor, or attempts to be humorous, this book is intended and designed to provide valuable insight and information for the reader to acquire a fundamental understanding of current U.S. immigration policy as well as immigration law. With that explicit understanding hopefully in mind, the author's desire and intent is to present a broad overview of immigration issues in the United States, without any intent or desire whatsoever to provide specific legal and/ or immigration advice to the reader.

The reader is specifically and particularly advised to consult a qualified immigration attorney or other qualified attorney for specific answers to specific legal and/or immigration questions. Immigration law and policy are very serious, complex, and complicated subjects.

Nothing written or stated in this book is intended or designed in any way to diminish, malign, or disparage any person, group, country, organization, institution, or people. Everyone is loved and respected. No one is despised or rejected. This book also includes **"Fifteen (15) Tips for Winning Immigration Cases."**

Reference is made to two books for the reader's additional interest: *Nothing Is Too Late*, by Mark E. Kalmansohn, 2004, www.brasseysinc.com, pages 6-7, 95, 185-186, 208, 237; and *Understanding The Law: A Primer*, by Attorney Charles Jerome Ware, 2008, www. iuniverse.com, www.amazon.com.

I want to take this opportunity to thank Linda Gale Brown-Smith for her exceptional assistance with this manuscript. This is the second book that Linda has assisted me with; the first was "Understanding the Law: A Primer" (November 2008). She is a partner with Christian Brown Associates which owns www.ourchanceforlove. com social networking site.

It is with every good, sincere, and earnest wish that this book will be of assistance, help and value to the reader in this complex arena of immigration law, policy, and practice.

To my wonderful wife, Fran, and my precious daughter, Lucinda-Marie.

Contents

Author's Note v

CHAPTER ONE: Immigration Humor 1

CHAPTER TWO: Native Americans 8

CHAPTER THREE: Black American Indians 13

CHAPTER FOUR: Beringia and the Bering Strait . 17

CHAPTER FIVE: Mariel: The Cuban Boatlift Crisis 21

CHAPTER SIX: The Cuban Immigration Paradox . . 28

CHAPTER SEVEN: The Haitian Immigration
    Paradox 33

CHAPTER EIGHT: Cubans versus Haitians: Disparate
    Immigration Treatment? 40

CHAPTER NINE: Getting Asylum 43

CHAPTER TEN: The Curious Case of "Joc Joc" . . . 51

CHAPTER ELEVEN: A Primer on "Temporary
    Protected Status" (TPS) 55

CHAPTER TWELVE: The "Green Card" is Not
    Green 61

CHAPTER THIRTEEN: The United States
    Immigration Judge 71

CHAPTER FOURTEEN: The United States Citizen
    and Immigration Service (USCIS) 77

CHAPTER FIFTEEN: Fundamentals of Immigration and Naturalization Law.................... 82

CHAPTER SIXTEEN: What is an "Illegal Alien," exactly?................................. 92

CHAPTER SEVENTEEN: A Summary of Immigration Law in the United States......... 95

CHAPTER EIGHTEEN: American Immigration in the "Post – 9/11/2001" Environment........ 108

CHAPTER NINETEEN: The USA Patriot Act of 2001................................. 113

CHAPTER TWENTY: American Immigration and The USA Patriot Act of 2001.................. 122

CHAPTER TWENTY-ONE: Current Immigration Issues in the United States................. 130

CHAPTER TWENTY-TWO: Fifteen (15) Tips for Winning Immigration Cases................ 138

ABOUT THE AUTHOR 145

INDEX.................................. 146

CHAPTER ONE:
Immigration Humor

"Laughter is the sun that drives winter from the human face."

— *Victor Hugo*

Like most humor, jokes about immigrants can be cutting. Unfortunately.

As I recall, the following joke made it into the internet humor database in 2005 in Great Britain:

> A Somalian arrives in Leicester as a new immigrant to the United Kingdom. He stops the first person he sees walking down the street and says, "Thank you Mr. Englishman for letting me in this country!" But the passerby says, "You are mistaken, I am an Albanian."
>
> The man goes on and encounters another passerby. "Thank you for having such a beautiful country here in Britain!" The person says, "I am from Bulgaria, not England."
>
> The new arrival walks further, and the next person he sees he stops, shakes his hands and says "Thank you for the wonderful Britain!" That person puts up his hand and says, "I am from Iran, I am not British!"

He finally sees a nice lady and asks suspiciously, "Are you a British citizen?" She says, "No, I am from Romania!"

So he is puzzled, and asks her, "Where are all the British?"

The Romanian lady looks at her watch, shrugs, and says... "Probably at work."

This same theme, that citizens are "paying for the welfare of immigrants," evolved into an American version of the story and surfaced on the internet "Thought Crime: Immigration Humor" blog in 2007:

A Somalian arrives in Minneapolis as a new immigrant to the United States. He stops the first person he sees walking down the street and says, "Thank you Mr. American for letting me in this country, giving me housing, food stamps, free medical care, and free education!" The passerby says, "You are mistaken, I am Mexican."

The man goes on and encounters another passerby. "Thank you for having such a beautiful country here in America!" The person says, "I not American, I Vietnamese."

The new arrival walks further, and the next person he sees he stops, shakes his hand and says, 'Thank you for the wonderful America!" That person puts up his hand and says, "I am from Bangladesh, I am not American!"

He finally sees a nice lady and asks, "Are you an American?" She says, No, I am from Israel!"

Puzzled, he asks her, "Where are all the Americans?"

The Jewish lady checks her watch and says... "Probably at work."

Generally, this type of humor presents an inaccurate or erroneous portrait of the existence of most immigrants; certainly in the United States where most new residents work for a living and contribute valuably to society. Of course, as always in any large group of people, there are exceptions. It has been reported that the proportion of immigrant-headed households using at least one major welfare program is thirty-three percent, compared to nineteen percent for native households [Center for Immigration Studies, 2007]. Further it is stated that the poverty rate for immigrants and their American born children under the age of eighteen is about seventeen percent, which is nearly fifty percent higher than the rate for so-called natives and their children [CIS, 2007]. The primary reason, however, for the high rates of immigrant poverty, lack of health insurance, and welfare use is actually their overall lower education levels, and certainly not their legal status or any unwillingness to work.

The U.S. Mexican border has become a hot topic in recent years in immigration debates. The humor on this topic, though, has come primarily from late-night comics:

– "President Bush called for the National Guard to patrol the U.S./Mexican border. The guards will track down and find illegals. That's not their job. They're trained to defend our country – not track down and find people. Let's be honest, the Guard couldn't even track down and find President Bush when he was in the National Guard." – Jay Leno

–"The United States Senate today took some steps to keep illegal immigrants out of our 'American Idol' competitions. They voted to build a 370-mile long fence along the border between the U.S. and Mexico. They also announced that they're going to hire illegal immigrant workers to build it. … The Senators voted overwhelmingly for the fence. As I said, it is 370 miles long. Unfortunately, the actual border with Mexico is more than 2,000 miles long. So, I guess the message is 'go around.' … Tentatively, they're calling it 'The Great Wall of Chimichanga'" – Jimmy Kimmel

–"The Mexican border will now have surveillance cameras and motion detectors. Our borders will be as secure as The Gap." – David Letterman

While some of us may laugh or smile at this humor, it is also important to note the sentiment of many as articulated by U.S. present William Jefferson Clinton in his 1998 commencement speech at Portland State University. In his commencement address, Clinton expressed strong support for immigrants to the United States, declaring: "America has wave after wave of immigrants … They (immigrants) have proved to be the most restless, the most adventurous, the most innovative, [and] the most industrious of people" [See, *Immigration*, by Mary E. Williams (San Diego: Green Haven Press) 2004].

Though U.S. presidents are customarily blamed for our nation's immigration woes, it should be noted that as a general principle the United States Congress has complete authority over immigration law. Normally, Presidential immigration power does not go beyond refugee policy.

Even though immigration to the United States has risen dramatically over the last century or so, the foreign-born share of America's population was still higher, for example, in 1900 [it was 20%] than it is today [it's about 10%]. There are a number of factors that may contribute to the decrease in the representation of foreign-born residents in our country. Probably the most important contributing factor has been the change in the composition of immigrants in terms of race and country of origin. Also see, <u>infra</u>, "Fifteen (15) Tips for Winning Immigration Cases."

Prior to 1890 or so, about 82% of immigrants to the U.S. came from northern and western Europe. Then, from about 1891 to around 1920, that number of immigrants dropped to about twenty-five percent. During this latter period, immigrants from eastern, central and southern Europe dominated the migration to the tune of about 64 percent. Considerable animosity greeted these different and foreign-born immigrants, resulting in substantial Federal legislation to limit immigration.

Top Ten Foreign Countries – Foreign Born
Population Among U.S. Immigrants
(2000, 2004, and 2010)

Country	#/year	2000	2004	2010	2010%
Canada	24,200	678,000	774,800	920,000	2.3%
China	50,900	1,391,000	1,594,600	1,900,000	4.7%
Cuba	14,800	952,000	1,011,200	1,100,000	2.7%
Dominican Republic	24,900	692,000	791,600	941,000	2.3%
El Salvador	33,500	765,000	899,000	1,100,000	2.7%
India	59,300	1,007,000	1,244,200	1,610,000	4.0%
Korea	17,900	701,000	772,600	880,000	2.2%
Mexico	175,900	7,841,000	8,544,600	9,600,000	23.7%
Philippines	47,800	1,222,000	1,413,200	1,700,000	4.2%
Vietnam	33,700	863,000	997,800	1,200,000	3.0%
Total Pop. Top 10	498,900	16,112,000	18,747,600	21,741,000	53.7%
Total Foreign Born	940,000	31,100,000	34,860,000	40,500,000	100%

[Historical Data from 2000 U.S. Census and 2004 Yearbook of Immigrant Statistics]

The U.S. Congress, in its role of possessing virtually complete authority over immigration, typically considers a wide range of immigration issues. Now that the number (but not percentage) of foreign-born residents of the nation is at the highest point in U.S. history, the debates over immigration policies grow continually in importance [In 2002, 32.5 million foreign-born residents were reported in the U.S.; Source: CRS Report for Congress, Order Code RS 20916, The Library of Congress, May 20, 2003].

Long before the Europeans and other immigrants arrived in North America, however, there were Native Americans.

CHAPTER TWO:
Native Americans

"Common sense and a sense of humor are the same thing, moving at different speeds. A sense of humor is just common sense, dancing."

— *William James*

For My People

Four men gather on the top of a 40-story building: an African-American, a Japanese, an American Indian, and a White man.

The African-American guy says, "This is for my brothers and sisters … for my people!" and he jumps off the building.

The Japanese guy says, "This, too, is for my people!", and he jumps off.

The American Indian says, "This is definitely for my people," and he immediately pushes the White man off the building.

Big Chief's Amazing Memory

An Australian travel writer touring western United States was checking out of the Dodge

City Hilton, and as he paid his bill said to the manager, "By the way, what's with the Indian chief sitting in the lobby? He's been there ever since I arrived."

"Oh, that's Big Chief Forget-me Not," said the manager. "The hotel is built on an Indian reservation, and part of the agreement is to allow the chief free use of the premises for the rest of his life. He is known as 'Big Chief Forget-me Not" because of his phenomenal memory. He is 92 and can remember the slightest details of his life."

The travel writer took this in, and as he was waiting for his cab decided to put the chief's memory to the test.

"G'dye, myte"! said the Aussie, receiving only a slight nod in return. "What did you have for breakfast on your 21st birthday?"

"Eggs, was the chief's instant reply, without even looking up, and indeed the Aussie was impressed.

He went off on his travel writing itinerary, right across to the east coast and back, telling others of Big Chief Forget-Me-Not's great memory. (One local noted to him that 'How' was a more appropriate greeting for an Indian chief than 'G'dye myte.')

On his return to the Dodge City Hilton eighteen months later, he was surprised to see 'Big Chief

Forget-me Not' still standing in the lobby, fully occupied with whittling away on a stick.

"How," said the Aussie.

"Scrambled," said the Chief.

Long before the "white man," or "Europeans," set foot on American soil, the American Indians, or *Native Americans*, had been living here. Though still debated, a currently accepted North American "new world" migration model places a migration of Native American ancestors from Euroasia to North America by way of Beringia around 20,000 to 30,000 years ago. Beringia was the land bridge which formerly connected the two continents of Euroasia and North America across what is now called the Bering Strait between Russia and Alaska.

Upon the eventual arrival of the Europeans to North America, it is estimated by some authorities that there were possibly over ten million Indians living north of present-day Mexico. The oldest documented Indian cultures in North America are Sandia (around 15000 BC), Clovis (about 12000 BC), and Folsom (about 8000 BC).

It should be noted that, even though it is believed that the American Indians originated in Asia many centuries ago, few if any of them actually came from India. Popular belief is that the name "Indian" was first used to identify them by one Christopher Columbus, who believed (apparently mistakenly) that the mainland and islands of America were part of the Indies, in Asia. When Columbus landed on the island of San Salvador in 1492 he was welcomed by a brown-skinned race of people whose physical appearance, in his opinion, caused him to believe that he had at least reached the country of India. He, therefore, called these people "Indios," or Indians. Despite wide-spread criticism, the name has stuck.

By definition, Native Americans in the United States, or American Indians, are the indigenous people from the regions of North America now encompassed by the continental United States, including parts of Alaska and the island state of Hawaii. These Americans consist of a large number of distinct tribes, states, territories, and ethnic groups. Many of these tribes of Indians survive as intact political communities.

Though once believed to have numbers in the millions, Native Americans (American Indians) now make up less than one percent of the total U.S. population. They do, however, represent half the languages and cultures in the nation, and include over 500 different groups representing geographic, language, socioeconomic, educational, spiritual and cultural diversity.

There are presently about 2.5 million "American Indian and Alaska Native" persons identified and registered with the U.S. Census Bureau.

Unfortunately, gambling is the only way many people become aware of American Indians. It has become a leading industry through casinos operated by several Native American governments within the United States. On the positive side, gambling revenues in several American Indian communities are being used as leverage to build more diversified economies within these communities. A significant number of Native American tribes, however, have declined to participate in the gambling industry for a number of reasons, including their concern for protection of their cultural values.

"Special" Status

The relationship between Native Americans (American Indians) and the United States of America today has been described as "special." American Indians are located in their own nations, tribes, or bands which have sovereignty or independence to a degree from the United States government. The Theory is that their societies are permitted to exist and hopefully flourish within the larger *immigrant* populations of Europeans, Hispanics, Asians, Middle Easterners, Africans, *et al.*

American Indians, or Native Americans, who were not already U.S. citizens as granted by other provisions of law such as with a previous treaty term (there have been numerous treaties with the American Indians, many of which have been broken by the United States) were granted citizenship in 1924 by the Congress of the United States.

And, yes, there were indeed Black American Indians; and still are in America.

CHAPTER THREE: Black American Indians

"Man, when you lose your laugh you lose your footing."

— Ken Kesey

Navajo Wisdom

About 1969 or so, a NASA (National Aeronautics and Space Administration) team doing work for the Apollo moon mission took the astronauts near Tuba City where the terrain of the Navajo Reservation looks very much like the lunar surface.

Along with all the trucks and large vehicles, there were two large figures dressed in full lunar spacesuits.

Nearby, a Black Navajo sheep herder and his son were watching the strange creatures walk about, occasionally being tended by personnel. The two Navajo people were noticed and approached by the NASA personnel. Since the man did not know English, his son asked for him what the strange creatures were and the NASA people told them that they are just men that are getting ready to go to the moon. The man became very excited and asked if he could send a message to the moon with the astronauts.

The NASA personnel thought this was a great idea so they rustled up a tape recorder. After the man gave them his message, they asked his son to translate. His son would not.

Later, they tried a few more people on the reservation to translate and every person they asked would chuckle and then refuse to translate. Finally, with cash in hand, someone translated the meaning, "Watch out for these guys, they come to take your land."

Most unfortunately, interracial relationships between American Indians and American Blacks have been an important perspective of American history that has been neglected (Dempsey, Mary, "The Indian Connection," American Visions (1996). One of the earliest recollections of African and Native American contact occurred in April 1502, when kidnapped African slaves were brought to the island of Hispaniola, which lies between the islands of Cuba to the west and Puerto Rico to the east. The Republic of Haiti now occupies the western third of the island and the Dominican Republic covers the eastern two-thirds of the island.

Christopher Columbus first arrived on the island in western Hispaniola, which is present-day Haiti, on or about December 5, 1492. On Columbus' second voyage to the eastern part of the islands, which is present-day Dominican Republic, in 1493, he founded the first Spanish colony in the "New World."

In any event, at some point shortly after April 1502, some of the African slaves escaped captivity and somewhere inland on the island started the first colony of African-Native Americans.

Later, in or about 1526, another group of African slaves escaped from their European slave master colonists in what is now South Carolina, and joined in with the local Indian population [Dirks, Dr. Jerald F., "Muslims in American History"]. Numerous contacts and relations between Black Americans and Indian Americans followed.

These historical relationships between American Indians and American Blacks run deep, both positively and negatively.

European slave-owning colonists went so far as to create treaties with Native American tribes urging them to return any runaway slaves. Many of them did so; many did not. The British Governor of New York, for example, in 1726 extracted a promise from the Iroquis Indians to return all runaway slaves who had joined their tribes. The same kind of promise was made by the Huron Indians in 1764, and was exacted from the Delaware Indians in 1765.

Many African Americans and Indian Americans married. Yet, some individual Indians in some tribes such as the Cherokee, owned African slaves. This could be expected or explained at the time because it was the institution of slavery that brought these Africans to America. In the end, even though less than three percent of Native Americans owned slaves, this difficult issue created damaging divides in their villages.

Intermarriage between African slaves and Native Indians began occurring on a more regular basis in the early 1600s in the so-called "Upper South." In 1622 Native Indians attacked the European colony of Jamestown (Virginia). They overran the colony, brought African slaves back to their communities, and gradually integrated them into their tribes [Katz, William Loren, "Africans and Indians: Only in America" (1997)].

But before there were Black Indians...

And, before there were Native Americans...

Prior to the arrival of Europeans...

And, in advance of the Northern migration of Americans and other Latin Americans...

There were Beringia and the subsequent Bering Strait.

CHAPTER FOUR: Beringia and the Bering Strait

Do not harm your neighbor, for it is not him you wrong, but yourself.

— *The Shawnee*

Cold War Humor

Millions of people living in Romania are escaping from dictator Ceauşescu's cruel regime. After millions of immigrants have rushed out of the country, the communist party's central committee decides to convince its people not to immigrate. Even more people, living in Romania are being persuaded to call their already immigrated relatives back to the country.

The idea is to get as many new communities as possible.

A jobless citizen is brought to the communist party's headquarters and asked: "Do you have relatives in the west?"

He replies: "Sure I have!" Then he's questioned further.

Communists: "Whom do you have in foreign countries?"

Citizen: "My brother lives in France"...

Communists: "What is his work there?"

Citizens: "He's a cook!"

Communists: "Great! Bring him back, we need a cook! Do you have any other relatives?"

Citizens: "I have a sister in Germany."

Communists: "What is her work?"

Citizens: "Typewriter."

Communists: "Wonderful, we just need a typewriter! Any other relatives?"

Citizens: "I have an uncle in Italy."

Communists: "What does he do there?"

Citizens: "He is a shoemaker."

Communists: "We were just looking for a shoemaker! Bring him back too! Whom else do you have abroad?"

Citizens: "I have a cousin in the USA."

Communists: "What does he do there?"

Citizens: "He doesn't. He's unemployed."

Communists: "Great! Bring him back and we'll make him communist party member!"

Citizens: "Are you crazy? He keeps us all alive!"

Though debated in academic circles, a currently accepted theory of North American "new world" migration contends a migration of Native American ancestors from Eurasia to North America by way of Beringia around 20,000 to 30,000 years ago.

Beringia, the so-called "Bering land bridge," was a natural bridge of land approximately a thousand miles from south to north at its greatest distance. The land covered the space between Asia and North America, and it joined present-day Alaska with eastern Siberia (of Russia) at various time periods during the Pleistocene ice ages.

Beringia was not a glacier, and was not glaciated. Since snowfall was very light during the times because of the mild southwesterly winds from the Pacific Ocean and lost their moisture over the fully glaciated Alaska Range. It is theorized that a small human population of a few thousand people survived the Last Glacial period in the grassland area of Beringia, and were isolated from their ancestor populations in Asian for at least five thousand years.

At some point later, this group expanded southward and easterly to populate the Americas. This may have happened around 16,500 years ago; about the time the American glaciers blocking their path southward began to melt. The Bering Strait was thus formed, with the former Beringia as the shallow land base.

The Bering Strait is comprised of the Chukchi Sea to the north and the Bering Sea to the south, and situated just to the south of the Arctic Circle. This shallow sea of water separates the current United States (Alaska) and

Russia (Siberia) by only 58 miles, and has a water depth of only 100 to 165 feet at its deepest points.

The Straight is named for Danish-born Russian mariner Vitus Bering, who is credited with spotting the Alaskan mainland while exploring the area with an expedition of Russian sailors in the mid-18th century. Due to the remarkably short distance between the two continents, in the last few decades adventurous and forward thinking engineers have discussed and considered the major construction project of either building a bridge over the 58-mile Straight or digging a tunnel beneath it. Financial and weather concerns have continually been major obstacles to construction.

Despite the enormously high costs that potentially would be involved in constructing a roadway between the United States and Russia, the concept remains an exciting one for many people on both sides of the border. The probability of such cooperation between the United States and a Russian ally, Cuba, remains remote however.

Remember the Cuban Boatlift Crisis?

CHAPTER FIVE:
Mariel: The Cuban Boatlift Crisis

In 1980, as a U.S. Immigration Judge appointed in the Administration of President Jimmy Carter, I was privileged to serve an assignment as a judge in exclusion and deportation hearings for the Cuban Boatlift Project, also known as the "Mariel Boat Lift." Humor exists in and about all countries and cultures, including Cuba and Cubans. Some examples follow.

Communist Cuba Joke

One Cuban young woman complains to another. "He lied to me! He told me that he was a luggage handler! It turns out, he's nothing but a neurosurgeon!"

Late Night Castro Humor

"Castro took over in 1959. He's the longest reigning dictator in power currently, if you don't count Martha Stewart. He's going to be 80 years old. He's talking about retiring. You know what that means? He could wind up in Miami." — Jay Leno, NBC Comedian

— "Now is the time to invade Cuba, America.

My proposal is controversial but we've invaded for less. Now I know our troops are tied up in Iraq so here's my plan. We harness the regime-destroying power of tourism. First, we send a fleet of Carnival cruise ships stuffed with battle-fattened early-retired middle-management types, their girth easily overpowering the frail bean-fed Cubans. Of course, there's nothing American tourists like more than things they can get at home. So in phase two Marine choppers air-drop an outlet mall, Old Navy, Sunglass Hut. Name brands here, maybe a Jamba Juice, Cinnabon. The Cubans will quickly become addicted to the easy American dollar. Communism will fail. And then we can finally allow Cuba to become a valuable trading partner like Communist China. So here's to freedom and the Havana Applebee's Cubanos. And what better way to celebrate than with a genuine 'Dominican' cigar. I can't wait until this 'Dominican' cigar is legal." — Stephen Colbert, Comedy Channel"

Cuban (Inside) Humor

One dark night, outside the small town of Medley, Florida, a fire started inside a local chemical plant and in a blink of an eye it exploded into massive flames. The alarm went out to all the fire departments for miles around. (Ft. Lauderdale, Davie, Hollywood, etc.) When the volunteer fire fighters appeared on the scene, the chemical company president rushed to the fire chief and said, "All of our secret formulas are in the vault. They must be saved. I will give $50,000 to the fire department that brings them out intact." But the roaring flames held the firefighters off.

Soon more fire departments had to be called in (West Palm, Boca, Miami) as the situation became more desperate. As the firemen arrived, the president shouted out that the offer was now $100,000 to the fire department who could bring out the company's secret files. From the distance, a lone siren was heard as another fire truck came into sight. It was the nearby Hialeah Volunteer Fire Company composed mainly of Cubans over the age of 65. To everyone's amazement, the little rundown fire engine, operated by these Cubans, passed all the newer sleek engines parked outside the plant...and drove straight into the middle of the inferno.

Outside, the other firemen watched as the Cuban old timers jumped off almost inside the flames and began to fight the fire with a performance and effort never seen before. Within a short time, the old timers had extinguished the fire and saved the secret formulas. The grateful chemical company president joyfully announced that for such a superhuman feat he was upping the reward to $200,000, and walked over to personally thank each of the brave, though elderly, Cuban firefighters. Channel 6, 7, 10, 23 and 51 TV news reporters rushed in after capturing the event on film asking, "What are you going to do with all that money?"

"Well," said the 70-year-old fire chief, "the first thing we're going to do is fix the brakes on that darn truck!"

This last joke could apply to many cultures, including Blacks, Europeans, Asians, Hispanics, *et al.*

The Cuban Boatlift, or "Mariel Boat Lift," however, was no laughing matter; particularly for the Cuban victims. I was there. I remember it well.

The Mariel Boat Lift was a mass movement of Cubans which officially began on April 15, 1980 and ended on October 31, 1980. At its end, over 125,000 Cubans had arrived in Southern Florida from Cuba's Mariel Harbor.

This mass exodus of Cubans was initially caused by a steep decline in the fragile Cuban economy, which subsequently led to heated internal problems on the island. Then, at a point, over 10,000 dissatisfied Cubans laid siege to the Peruvian Embassy seeking asylum.

Eventually, under tremendous duress, the Cuban government declared that anyone who desired to leave the country could do so. A quick exodus was organized by Cuban-American groups with the grudging agreement of Cuban President Fidel Castro. But the wily Castro had some tricks up his sleeve. The crafty dictator opened up his jails and mental health facilities and released thousands of those Cuban residents into the mix of the departing refugees. This malicious act by the Cuban President caused severe political problems for U.S. President Jimmy Carter. The migration was ended by mutual agreement of the two countries in October 1980.

Background for the Mariel Boatlift

Roots for the Boatlift go back to 1977, in the early days of the Administration of new U.S. President Jimmy Carter. The new President came into office wanting to improve relations with Cuba. The Administration quickly established an Interest Section through the State

Department in Havana, Cuba, and Castro's Cuban government in turn created an Interest Section in Washington, D.C. Shortly thereafter, Cuba agreed to the release of several dozen political prisoners.

In November 1978, the Castro government held a meeting in Havana with a group of Cubans living in exile. Out of that meeting came the decision, among others, by the Cuban government to start allowing Cuban exiles to visit their relatives in Cuba as soon as January 1979.

In May of 1979, several Cuban citizens used a bus to crash through the gates of the Embassy of Venezuela in the upscale Havana suburb of Miramar. They were seeking political asylum. This was the beginning of several occasions of forced entry by disgruntled Cubans into the embassies of Peru and Venezuela in 1979 and early 1980 seeking political asylum. Since the general Cuban population did not have access to any embassy or foreign mission without express consent of the Cuban government authorities, the use of buses, cars and trucks as battering rams to break into foreign missions was common.

Originally, from an immigration perspective, the Carter Administration was magnanimous and had an "open-arms" immigration policy regarding Cubans. Cubans were immediately granted refugee status and all the legal rights that came with refugee status. The American public's initial reaction to this policy towards Cuban immigrants was favorable.

During the course of the Mariel Boatlift, however, the public's view changed. With Cuban President Fidel Castro's constant public declarations that those who were leaving Cuba for the United States were "Lumpens" and the "scum of the Cuban society," in combination with reports that many of the refugees had been released from Cuban prisons and insane asylums, the American public increasingly changed its opinion and viewed the refugees as "undesirable immigrants."

This change in the American public's view of these Cuban refugees was made even more devastating by the history of immigration law in the United States. It is important to observe that up until about the late 1800's the United States was essentially an open border country with minimal, if any real, immigration laws. Then, in or about 1882, the U.S. Congress placed a so-called "head tax" on all immigrants; barring from admission to this country so-called "idiots, lunatics, convicts, and persons likely to become a public charge." These restrictions still exist to this day, as Fidel Castro was perfectly aware.

Cuban Immigrant Arrivals on the Beaches of South Florida (Miami) during the Mariel (Cuban) Boatlift, by Month (1980)

Month (1980)	Arrivals (#)	Arrivals (%)
April (from April 21)	7665	6%
May	86488	69%
June	20800	17%
July	2629	2%
August	3939	3%
September	3258	3%
Total	124779	100%

Source: U.S. Coast Guard data.

The Cuban Boatlift was a crisis of monumental proportions...and a paradox.

CHAPTER SIX:
The Cuban Immigration Paradox

To its credit, Cuba has a comparatively good reputation for its health system and education programs. In particular, efforts are made early to instill values of respect, courtesy and good manners in young students. The story of Ramon and the school teacher is instructive.

Ramon and the School Teacher

A schoolteacher in Havana asked her class, "If the sea between Cuba and Miami were to dry up, how long would it take to walk across?"

When she got no response, she asked Ramon to give an answer. After a moment of thought, he said, "Forty days."

The teacher was naturally surprised. "Pepito," she said, "the distance from Havana to Miami is only about ninety miles. Maybe I didn't make the question clear. Pretend that it's all smooth and level ground. NOW how long would it take?

Ramon insisted however on his answer of forty days.

"But why?" asked the teacher.

"Well, because you would constantly have to say, 'Excuse me,' 'Pardon me please,' 'Excuse me, sir.' Pardon me Miss,' 'Excuse me...'"

It is pretty clear that President Jimmy Carter, a humanitarian, allowed the Mariel Boatlift, also nicknamed the "Freedom Flotilla," for humanitarian and political reasons. On May 11, 1980, a single day, 4,588 "Marielitos" or Cuban refugees sailed by way of shrimp boats and other small vessels to U.S. shores at Miami. In the end, the 125,000 "Marielitos" who came accounted for about 1.3 percent of the Cuban nation's population at that time.

The refugees were granted parole status, which allowed them to live in the United States. However, pursuant to the unusual circumstances of their arrival here, they were not considered to have "officially" entered the country. In essence, for immigration law purposes, they occupied a legal "twilight zone" or "neutral status." Odd, for sure. Later, after routine processing by the Immigration and Naturalization Services (INS) under the Immigration Reform and Control Act of 1986, most of the refugees were eventually granted permanent resident status.

The "undesirables" issue was a problem, though.

It is clear that the vast majority of the "Marielitos" had been law-abiding citizens in Cuba, or otherwise were legitimate "political prisoners" within the meaning and context of INS policies and procedures. That is, these "political prisoners" only crime had been to oppose Fidel Castro's communist regime. But, some of them suffered very serious mental illness, and an even larger number of the refugees had been convicted of being serious criminals whose offenses warranted continued detention and subsequent removal from the United States. Further, many others in the group were detained and targeted for removal for a variety of reasons such as committing serious crimes on American soil after their arrival and before their parole status could be adjusted to permanent residency.

At some point relatively early in the massive migration it began to be revealed that a number of the "Marielitos" were part of a malicious scheme by Fidel Castro to get rid of his Cuban "undesirables" and pawn them on America. It was an unfortunate and undeserved blow to the humanitarian President Jimmy Carter.

Americans, generally, were outraged. Cuban Americans, particularly, were angry.

Ultimately, approximately 3,700 of the refugees were deemed excludable and deportable aliens after hearings by the Immigration and Naturalization Service (INS). I was one of those immigration judges who presided over many of those 22,000 or so exclusion and deportation hearings.

Even so-called "illegal aliens" have rights under the United States Constitution.

Excludable aliens, however, unlike so-called "illegal aliens," are not considered to be "persons" under the United States Constitution and consequently have no legal rights here. Good faith efforts were made by the Carter Administration to send the excludable (undesirable) refugees back to Cuba, but Castro refused to repatriate or accept those Cuban nationals. Ultimately, about 2,300 of the excludable aliens were shipped to two U.S. prisons: one a regular prison in Oakdale, Louisiana; and the second, a maximum-security prison in Atlanta, Georgia that had once housed the infamous gangster Al Capone.

It was this infamous federal penal institution in Atlanta in which I presided over most of my exclusion and deportation hearings as an INS Judge pursuant to Section 101 and 103 of the Immigration and Nationality Act, 28 CFR 0.105, and 8 CRF 2.1.

These "undesirables" spawned numerous articles and books, and even movies; the most famous being the extremely violent 1983 motion picture *Scarface*. In the movie, actor Al Pacino plays a cocaine-addicted, extremely violent Cuban marielito. This unfortunate and negative stereotype has persisted for years.

The excludable Marielitos remained jailed in federal prison in Louisiana and Georgia, with no right of legal counsel, for about seven years, until 1987. As I recall, in my INS court, represented several of the Marielitos were represented by legal counsel.

In November 1987, a sudden change in relations between the United States and Cuba brought movement to their existence. The two countries reached an agreement designed to control the movement of Cubans into the United States. The agreement established an annual quota of 20,000 Cuban immigrants into the United States as long as Fidel Castro agreed to repatriate the Mariel excludables whose names had been listed in 1984. The American immigration process and our immigration laws had to be respected and followed, however.

31

Consistent with American immigration laws at that time, priority was given to former Cuban political prisoners and their relatives. Those Cubans who for many different reasons could not wait to leave Castro's regime took to the seas in small boats and attempted to by-pass the U.S. immigration process. They were detained, and upon learning that they would be returned to Cuba they rioted in their detention camps.

Riot negotiations were held with the U.S. Department of Justice and the rioters. The Department of Justice promised "fair and equitable" hearings to review each case on the merits. Those refugees deemed harmless to U.S. society were released. This group amounted to several thousand. Others continued to be detained, including numbers of Haitian immigrants who also arrived during the Mariel Boatlift.

Finally, on January 12, 2005, almost twenty-five years after the Mariel Boatlift, the United States Supreme Court ruled in *Clark v. Martinez* that Cuban refugees Sergio Suarez Martinez and Daniel Benitez, and others similarly situated who have been deemed inadmissible aliens and are subject to removal but cannot be removed, can only be detained for a period of six months. The Supreme Court concluded that six months was a reasonable period of time in which removals from the United States should be implemented. With the Court's final decision in *Clark v. Martinez* that the continued detention of the Cubans was illegal, the U.S. Immigration service began quietly releasing the approximately 750 remaining detainees.

But wait! What about the Haitians?

CHAPTER SEVEN:
The Haitian Immigration Paradox

Haitian Proverb

"Dye mon, gen mon."

Beyond the mountain is another mountain.

(Haitian proverb of both patience and the recognition of how difficult life in Haiti is.)

Haitian Coffee

A young couple treated themselves to a meal in an expensive restaurant in Petionville, Haiti. After eating a huge meal they had settled back in their chairs to relax and chat. The waiter came along and asked: "Will you have American coffee or Haitian coffee?" The woman replied that she'd have American coffee, while the man chose Haitian coffee. The waiter said, "coming right up," and rushed off. "Ah," said the woman, this is a fantastic restaurant. The service is so solicitous and they have just everything." Her date agreed. After a few minutes the waiter returned with two cups, one small demitasse cup and one large coffee cup. He placed the large cup in front of the woman and the small cup in front of the man.

Then, with great ceremony, he filled both cups from the same coffee pot!

Cubans are not the only people to engage in modern-day boatlifts to the United States. Haitians have had several such mass arrivals to our shores. But, without the same results as Cubans. Unfortunately.

In the early 1970s, during the Republican Nixon Administration, Haitians started their migration by sea in almost anything floatable to south Florida. Like many others coming to the United States from southern neighbor countries, a significant number of them were unauthorized. Influential social and economic forces in the south Florida regions pressured the Federal Government to stop this "alien" population stream. And it did. [Mitchell, Christopher, "The Annals of the American Academy of Political and Social Science," Vol. 534, No. 1, 69-80 (1994)].

From the early 1970s to 1981, arriving Haitian "boat people" refugees were detained and held in south Florida camps. Most were eventually excluded and deported as quickly as possible. Despite Democratic President Jimmy Carter's instructions to his advisors in 1980 to develop immigration policies that treated Haitian and Cuban "boat people" the same, it did not happen.

Instead, starting in 1981 the Republican President Ronald Reagan Administration began using the U.S. Coast Guard to "intercept" the Haitians in their heavily-laden boats at sea and direct them back to Haiti. Then, in or about May 1992, the policy escalated to "interdicting" the small Haitian vessels and "escorting" them back to Haiti, without affording the refugee passengers any opportunity to even request political asylum or any other immigrant status in the United States. The Reagan Administration generally viewed Haitian boat people as "economic" migrants deserting one of the poorest countries in the world.

On the negative side, this policy against the Haitian refugees appeared clearly to be inhumane and discriminatory, and it properly aroused public condemnation. However, on the positive side, political criticism of these interception and interdiction policies has helped the U.S. Government "get off the fence" and act more in favor of a democratic regime in Haiti. Presumably, this political policy of supporting "democracy" in Haiti has helped the U.S. undercut the prevailing argument that Haitian boat people are, like the Cubans, fleeing political persecution in Haiti. In sum, from an immigration policy perspective, it supports the U.S. position of repatriation for Haitian refugees.

The Paradox of Humor

Haitian Woman:"I want asylum because I have run away from a dictator."

U.S. Immigration Officer: "Do you mean Haitian President Aristide?"

Haitian Woman: "No, I mean my mother-in-law. She's always telling me what to do. Please don't send me back. I would rather go to Cuba."

U.S. Immigration Officer: "Great idea! If you go to Cuba, then come here, we might let you stay."

It should be pointed out that the "Haitian President Aristide" referred to in the above paradox as humor story is Jean-Bertrand Aristide (born July 15, 1953). Aristide was a former Roman Catholic Church priest who was President of Haiti in 1991, and again from 1994 to 1996, and then again from 2001 to 2004.

There were at least four democratically elected leaders of Haiti before Aristide came along, including the infamous Francois Duvalier.

Haitian President Aristide was deposed twice, in a military coup in September 1991, and in a rebellion in February 2004. He alleged that he was kidnapped by the U.S. and Canadian military and forced into exile in South Africa. After being deposed a second time (even though he presented a signed resignation), Aristide argued from his exile in the Central African Republic that he was still the legal and legitimate president of Haiti, and that the United States military had kidnapped him. Another paradox.

United States Post-Mariel Policy on Haitians

As we know, the Mariel boatlift was essentially a mass exodus from Cuba and influx to the United States of asylum seekers during a seven-month period in 1980. Approximately 125,000 Cubans arrived by boats to the shores of south Florida. What you may not know is that an estimated 25,000 Haitians also were among the mass migration. The Haitians were not received in Miami as well as the Cubans.

Democratic President Jimmy Carter's Administration labeled the Cubans and Haitians who came during the 1980 Mariel Boatlift as "Cuban-Haitian Entrants." In doing so, the Administration also used its discretionary authority through the Attorney General of the United States (who was retired U.S. Court of Appeals judge Griffin Bell, from Georgia) to admit them.

Apparently, the vast majority of Haitians who arrived in the Miami area did not qualify for asylum according to the recently (1980)-enacted individualized definition of "persecution" in §§207-208 of the Immigration and Nationality Act (INA, as amended by the Refugee Act of 1980). The new definition stated that aliens must demonstrate a well-founded fear that if returned home, they will be "persecuted" based upon one of five characteristics: race, religion, nationality, membership in a particular social group, or their political opinion. Later, in 1986, an adjustment of status provision was included in the Immigration Reform and Control Act (IRCA) of 1986 that enabled most Cuban Entrants and a few Haitian Entrants to become legal permanent residents (LPRs).

Treatment of Haitian Immigrants Under the Homeland Security Act of 2002

In the "Post-9/11" environment, that is, after the terrorist attacks upon the United States on September 11, 2001, treatment of Haitian immigrants through the eight years of the Bush "43" Republican Administration did not improve. It remains to be seen how the Haitians will be treated through the Administration of America's forty-fourth President, Democrat Barack Obama.

The Homeland Security Act of 2002 (P.L. 107-296), among many other changes, effectively abolished the old Immigration and Naturalization Service (INS) and transferred its duties and responsibilities from the Attorney

Attorney Charles Jerome Ware

General and the U.S. Department of Justice to several bureaus within the brand new Department of Homeland Security (DHS). Thus making an even bigger mess of the government bureaucracy regarding immigration.

Within the new DHS, the responsibilities for Haitian immigrants are dispersed across the Department's bureau of the (i) Coast Guard *(interdiction)*, (ii) Customs and Border Protection *(apprehensions and inspections)*, (iii) Immigration and Customs Enforcement *(detention)*, (iv) Citizenship and Immigration Service *(credible fear determination)*, and (v) the Department of Justice's (DOJ's) Executive Office for Immigration Review *(asylum and removal hearings)*.

U.S. Coast Guard Interdiction of Haitians, 1982-2004

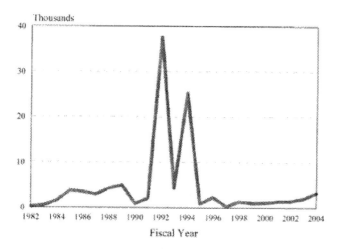

[SOURCES: United States Coast Guard Data; Congressional Research Service, The Library of Congress, 2005.]

38

The U.S. Coast Guard's interdiction of the Haitians, in contrast with America's general acceptance of the Cubans, has presented ongoing concerns among many of perceived disparate treatment.

CHAPTER EIGHT: Cubans versus Haitians: Disparate Immigration Treatment?

Is there disparate immigration treatment between Cubans and Haitians by the United States? Let us sort through this issue, if we can.

From an immigration policy perspective, both Cuba and Haiti are viewed as having a history of repressive governments with documented human rights violations. Both countries, too, have a history of off-loading asylum seekers to the U.S. by boats. And, though U.S. immigration law is alleged to generally apply neutrally without regard to any country of origin, there are indeed "special laws and agreements" concerning both Cuban and Haitian immigrants [See, Congressional Research Service (CRS) Report RL 32294, *Haiti: Developments and U.S. Policy Since 1991 and Current Congressional Concerns*, by Maureen Taft-Morales; and see, CRS Report LR 32730, *Cuba: Issues for the 109th Congress*, by Mark P. Sullivan, a discussion of United States – Cuba relations].

The Cuban Adjustment Act (CAA)

However, despite these points of similarity, the treatment of Cuban immigrants seeking asylum in the U.S. differs from Haitians fleeing their country. The fact is that Cubans receive more generous treatment under U.S. law than Haitians or, for that matter, foreign nationals from any other country. There is a law on the books that supports this policy-preference by the U.S. for Cubans. It is called the Cuban Adjustment Act (CAA) of 1966 (P.L. 89-732).

"Wet Foot/Dry Foot"

The Cuban Adjustment Act (CAA) of 1966, as amended, provides that certain Cubans who have been physically present in the United States for at least one year may adjust to permanent resident status at the discretion of the Attorney General. As a direct consequence or result of special migration agreements with Cuba, a "wet foot/dry foot" practice toward Cuban migrants has developed. Simply and plainly put, as you may have seen on television shows or in the movies featuring the shores and beaches of the Miami/South Florida area, Cubans who do not reach the dry land shore of the U.S. ("wet foot" Cuban immigrants) are interdicted and returned to Cuba unless they can cite and subsequently demonstrate fears of persecution. Those Cuban immigrants who successfully reach the shores or beaches of the U.S. ("dry foot" Cubans) are inspected for entry by the Department of Homeland Security (DHS) and generally permitted to stay in this country and adjust under the Cuban Adjustment Act (CAA) the following year.

Public Law 89

The Cuban Adjustment Act (CAA), Public Law Number 89-732, is a federal law enacted on November 2, 1966, during the Democratic Administration of President Lyndon Johnson. The law applies to any native or citizen of Cuba who has been immigrationally inspected and admitted into the United States, or paroled into the United States after January 1, 1959. Additionally, the Cuban native or citizen must have been physically present for at least one year in the United States, and is legal admissible to this country as a permanent resident.

In sum, the major provisions of P.L. 89 (CAA) were to change the legal status of the Cuban immigrants to the U.S.; to treat them as political refugees and thus grant them political asylum; and consequently provide them immediately with privileges that no other group of immigrants to the U.S. enjoys. These privileges include, among others, automatic permanent resident status (without the usual bureaucratic review and without the usual waiting time), the opportunity for these previously-illegal (undocumented) Cuban aliens to work legally, to receive government welfare, to be eligible for unemployment benefits, and to be eligible for free medical care: all of which are things the average immigrant is not eligible for.

There have been policy debates on the unequal or disparate treatment of asylum-seekers from Cuba and Haiti within U.S. Administrations since the enactment of the 1966 Cuban Adjustment Act. Clearly, the Act was debated vigorously during Democratic President Jimmy Carter's Administration; particularly in light of the Cuban (or "Mariel") Boatlift crisis. The Clinton Administration, in the 1990s, was able to garner some support and progress in aligning the arrivals of both Haitian and Cuban immigrants to virtually the same legal requirements with a perceived overall change of political policy toward Cuba. Today, in 2009, the imbalance in treatment remains, however,

CHAPTER NINE: Getting Asylum

During a visit to the mental asylum, a visitor asked the Director how do you determine whether or not a patient should be institutionalized. "Well," said the director, "we fill up a bathtub, then we offer a teaspoon, a teacup and a bucket to the patient and ask him to empty the bathtub." "Oh, I understand," said the visitor. "A normal person would use the bucket because it is bigger than the spoon or the teacup." "No" said the director, "A normal person would pull the plug...Do you want the bed near the window?"

Source: http://www.sheknowsbest.com/weekend-humor-mental-asylum

If you understand the above joke, you also probably understand that "mental asylum" is *not* the type of asylum we are discussing in this book on immigration. Surprisingly, many people do not understand the difference.

What is Asylum?

For immigration purposes, Asylum is a form of protection granted by the Government to individual applicants or aliens in the United States who can establish that they have been persecuted in their former country, or have legitimate fear that they will be persecuted in the former country on account of their race, religion, nationality, membership in a particular social group, or their political opinion. Alien applicants who meet this definition of a refugee, and who are already in the United States, or who are seeking entry into the United States at a legitimate port of entry may qualify for a grant of asylum and may be permitted to remain in this country as long as they are not barred or prohibited from either applying for or being granted asylum. Those applicants who are granted asylum are also eligible to make application for adjustment of their status to that of lawful permanent residence.

There are effectively and practically two ways of gaining asylum in the United States. They are the "affirmative asylum process" through the United States Citizenship and Immigration Services (USCIS), and the "defensive asylum process" with the Executive Office for Immigration Review (EOIR). Both processes, of course, involve the filing of forms.

Either way, whether "affirmative" or "defensive," an alien or immigrant may apply for Asylum regardless of his or her immigration status; in other words, whether they are in the United States lawfully or unlawfully.

"Affirmative" Asylum Processing with the United States Citizenship and Immigration Services (USCIS)

Aliens or immigrants who are already physically present in the United States, regardless of how they arrived and/or irrespective of their current immigration status, may apply for asylum in the affirmative asylum process. These applicants do so "affirmatively" by submitting their completed *Form I-589, Application for*

Asylum and for Withholding of Removal "without delay," meaning within one year from the date of their last arrival in the United States. Under this process, if these "genuine asylum seekers" cannot or do not present themselves to authorities within the one year period, they must show:

(1) Changed circumstances that materially affected their eligibility, or extraordinary circumstances relating to the delay in filing for asylum; and

(2) that the applicant for asylum filed within a reasonable amount of time given those changed or extraordinary circumstances.

Filing

Immigration, like many other areas of law and government, is form-driven. Applicants for Asylum should file the Form I-589 with a USCIS Service Center (preferably the Center nearest to them). All asylum applicants are interviewed. The policy is that these interviews should be non-adversarial and conducted by trained USCIS asylum officers at one of the eight (currently) Asylum Offices throughout the United States. The Asylum Office closest to the applicant's place of residence is usually chosen for the interview.

Timelines

Normal protocol and policy dictate that an "affirmative" asylum applicant is interviewed by USCIS officers within 43 days of application. It is then expected that a final decision on asylum will be "received" by the applicant within 14 days after the interview.

Should the applicant's case for asylum not be approved, and if he or she does not maintain a valid (lawful) immigration status, they are issued a Notice to Appear and their case is referred to an Immigration Judge (IJ) at the Executive Office for Immigration Review (EOIR) for what is called a *de novo* consideration of their application for asylum. In other words, the applicant's asylum case shifts from the "affirmative" asylum process with USCIS over to the "defensive" asylum process with EOIR.

Further, the applicant's asylum case processing may be extended or generally take longer to complete if the applicant's security or background checks are delayed for any reason. If the applicant does not live near one of the eight Asylum Offices and an Asylum Officer is required to travel to a USCIS field office to conduct the interview, it is almost certain that the process will be delayed. Generally, with the asylum programs of 1995 in place, case processing, including by the Immigration Judge at EOIR, is reportedly complete within about six (6) months of the initial application for asylum (i.e., filing of the Form I-59 at a USCIS Service Center).

Rights of Asylum Applicants

For the most part, asylum applicants are generally not authorized to work in the United States while their application is pending before the USCIS or the EOIR. Of course, there are exceptions to this rule. It should be noted, as well, that "affirmative" asylum applicants are rarely detained. Instead, they are generally free to live anywhere they can in the country pending the completion of their asylum process with the USCIS and, if found ineligible by USCIS, then during the "defensive" asylum process with EOIR.

"Defensive" Asylum Processing with the Executive Office for Immigration Review (EOIR)

United States Immigration Judges (IJs) with the Executive Office for Immigration Review (EOIR) preside over hearings on asylum applications only in the context of "defensive" asylum proceedings. In "defensive" asylum hearings, the applicant requests asylum as a *defense* against *removal* from the United States.

"Defensive" asylum cases are heard by Immigration Judges in *adversarial*, or court-room-styled, hearings or proceedings. As in other court-type proceedings, the Judge hears the evidence: the asylum applicant's claim and any arguments about the applicant's eligibility made by the Federal Government, which is represented by attorneys from the Immigration and Customs Enforcement (ICE). The Immigration Judge then makes an eligibility determination after considering all of the evidence.

If the applicant is found eligible, the Judge then orders that asylum be granted.

If the applicant is determined by the Judge to be ineligible for asylum, the Judge then determines whether the applicant is eligible for any other forms of immigration relief from removal. If so, the Judge will order such relief from removal. If not, the Judge will order the applicant removed from the United States.

The IJ's decision can be appealed to the Board of Immigration Appeals (BIA) by either the applicant or the Government. Appeal from the Board of Immigration Appeals may be made to a U.S. Court of Appeals.

Alien applicants for asylum are generally placed into "defensive asylum processing" in one of the following ways:

A. they are referred to an IJ by USCIS after a finding of ineligibility at the conclusion of the "affirmative" asylum process, or

B. they are placed in removal proceedings because they:

(1)   were apprehended in the United States or at a U.S. port-of-entry without prior legal documents or in violation of their status; or

(2)   were caught trying to enter the United States without prior documentation and were placed in the expedited removal process and found to have a credible fear of persecution or torture by an Asylum Officer.

Important Distinctions Between
"Affirmative" and "Defensive" Asylum Processes

Affirmative	Defensive
Asylum-seeker has not been placed in removal proceedings before an Immigration Judge	Asylum-seeker has been placed in removal proceedings before an Immigration Judge
Asylum-seeker affirmatively submits his or her asylum application to a USCIS Service Center	Asylum seeker: Is referred by an Asylum Officer. Is placed in removal proceedings for immigration violations; or Tried to enter the U.S. without proper documents and was found to have a credible fear of persecution or torture If the individual was referred by USCIS, the asylum application already filed with carry over to the IJ. If the individual did not yet submit an asylum application he will submit it to the IJ.
Asylum-seeker appears before a USCIS Asylum Officer for a non-adversarial interview	Asylum-seeker appears before an Immigration Judge with the Executive Office for Immigration Review for an adversarial court-like hearing
Applicant must provide a qualified translator for the asylum interview	The court provides applicant with a qualified interpreter for the immigration hearing

SOURCE: http://www.uscis.gov/portal/site/uscis/

It is important for the reader to understand that the standards for alien applicants to get or gain asylum are generally stringent. The applicant must establish "persecution" or "legitimate fear of persecution," not prosecution.

There is a difference. Take, for example, the curious case of *Joc Joc*.

CHAPTER TEN:
The Curious Case of "Joc Joc"

Remember: In asylum cases, the alien applicant must establish "persecution" or "legitimate fear of persecution," not prosecution or legitimate fear of prosecution.

Filipinos have an interesting reputation for using amusingly repetitious nicknames such as "Noy Noy," "Bong Bong," or "Say Say." But who exactly is "Joc Joc?"

This story on asylum applicant Jocelyn Bolante, also known as "Joc Joc," is probably apocryphal already in the annals of asylum applicants. We actually read about it first on the Internet [www.philippinenews.com/article].

Allegedly, a Philippine man by the name of Jocelyn Bolante, also nicknamed "Joc Joc," was a "fertilizer scam architect" in the Philippines. Apparently, while he was Undersecretary of the Philippine Department of Agriculture, he allegedly diverted government funds set-aside for the purchase of fertilizer to the Reelection Committee for Philippine President Arroyo. A no-no. He subsequently resigned his position with the Department of Agriculture.

Later, the Philippine Senate initiated an investigation into charges of corruption within the Department. Upon completion of the investigation, the group issued a report alleging that Joc Joc was the "architect" of the diversion of funds. The Senate also recommended that Joc Joc face criminal charges, along with Felix Montes, the Assistant Secretary of Agriculture.

During the Senate's investigation of the charges of corruption in the Agriculture Department, Joc Joc was subpoenaed to testify. He declined to do so. The Philippine Senate then issued a warrant for his arrest. Jocelyn Bolante, or "Joc Joc," left the Philippines for the United States.

When he arrived in the United States on July 7, 2006, Joc Joc was apparently unaware that his visa had been revoked by the U.S. Embassy in Manila. He was promptly denied entry into the U.S. and detained by the authorities for non-possession of a valid visa. As of this date, September 12, 2008, he has remained in custody of the U.S. Government.

Subsequent to his arrival and detention in the U.S., Joc Joc made application by way of the "defensive" asylum process with the Executive Office for Immigration Review (EOIR), seeking asylum and withholding of removal. He argued that he had been persecuted in his country of the Philippines, and that he had a legitimate fear that he would be persecuted if returned to the Philippines.

The Immigration Judge (IJ) did not buy Joc Joc's arguments. The Judge denied him the requested relief, holding in his decision that the "vague threats and opaque predictions of harm were insufficient to establish" Joc Joc's claims. The IJ also noted that the Philippine Senate's issuance of a subpoena to Joc Joc was intended to investigate and eventually *prosecute* him for alleged violations of Philippine laws, and <u>not</u> to *persecute* him on account of his political opinion or membership in a particular social group.

The Board of Immigration Appeals (BIA) affirmed the IJ's decision.

On appeal to the U.S. Court of Appeals for the Seventh Circuit, the Court rejected Joc Joc's claim that he feared persecution upon returning to the Philippines [*Jocelyn Bolante v. Attorney General Mukasey*, No. 07-2550, August 27, 2008, CA7]. The Court of Appeals concluded that Joc Joc did not demonstrate a well-rounded fear of such persecution. Instead, the appellate court noted somewhat sarcastically, Joc Joc's real fear was "fear of prosecution for his alleged role in [a] corruption scandal." In other words, his true fear was of prosecution, not of persecution.

The Seventh Circuit Court of Appeals stated in its opinion that "though prosecution can [indeed] become persecution, courts uniformly recognize that a foreign state's [such as the Philippines] prosecution of its citizens for violating its own laws does not automatically [without more evidence] equate with persecution."

Further, the court concluded:

"Prosecution for activities that would be illegal under our own laws is not grounds for asylum. Similarly, being suspected of a crime does not necessarily render an asylum applicant eligible for asylum. The court observed that Joc Joc "does not presently face prosecution. No charges have been filed against him, and although the Senate

Committee has recommended charges against Bolante, they have also recommended charges against Montes, who has yet to face prosecution. Other members of President Arroyo's government, including Montes, have testified before the Senate Committee on the Fertilizer Scam and have not yet been physically harmed or unjustly prosecuted." Montes even testified before the IJ. [*Bolante v. Mukasey*, No. 07-2550, 8/27/08, CA7].

CHAPTER ELEVEN: A Primer on "Temporary Protected Status" (TPS)

A girl and her mother, new TPS immigrants in the United States, were visiting a shopping center. Both were amazed by just about everything they saw, but particularly by two shiny, silver walls that could move apart and back together again.

The girl asked her mother: "What is this, Mom?" The mother (never having seen an elevator before) responded: "Dear, I have never seen anything like this in my life. I don't know what it is."

While the girl and her mother were watching wide-eyed, an old man in a wheel chair rolled up to the moving shiny, silver walls and pressed a button. The walls opened and the old man rolled his wheel chair between them and into a small room. The walls closed again; the girl and her mother watched small circles of lights with numbers above the walls light up. They continued to watch the circles light up in the reverse direction.

Finally, the shiny walls opened up again and a handsome, muscular and attractive young man stepped out. Like magic.

The mother shouts to her daughter: "GO GET YOUR FATHER!!!"

Cute story. And funny. However, the vast majority of TPS immigrants are not nearly as unsophisticated as this story may imply. Precisely what is TPS or Temporary Protected Status?

Temporary Protected Status, or TPS, is a temporary immigration status granted to certain eligible aliens who are nationals or citizens of certain designated countries who cannot return home because of a crisis in their home country (or parts thereof) that is recognized as such by section 244 of the Immigration and Nationality Act (INA); Immigration Act of 1990 ("IMMACT"), P.L. 101-649; *et al.*

Under the Act, Congress established a procedure which the Attorney General of the United States may provide TPS to certain aliens or immigrants in the United States who are temporarily unable to safely return to their home country due to:

(i)   ongoing armed conflict;

(ii) an environmental disaster; or

(iii) other   extraordinary   and   temporary conditions.

A TPS designation is generally effective for at least six (6) months; and may last usually for a maximum of eighteen (18) months. The TPS may, of course, be extended by the Secretary of Homeland Security. More about this in the "Change of Authority and Responsibility" section *infra.*

Change of Authority and Responsibility

On March 1, 2003, pursuant to the new Homeland Security Act of 2002, Public Law 107-296, there was a change of authority and responsibility for implementation of TPS. Responsibility and authority to designate a country (or parts thereof) for TPS, and to extend and terminate TPS designations, was changed or transferred from the Attorney of the United States to the Secretary of the Department of Homeland Security.

Concurrently, with the above-stated change, the responsibility for administering the TPS program was transferred from the former Immigration and Naturalization Service (the "Service") to the U.S. Citizenship and Immigration Services (USCIS), a component or department within the U.S. Department of Homeland Security (or "DHS").

Forms

The pertinent forms to file for TPS are (i) Form I-821, Application for Temporary Protected Status, and (ii) Form I-765, Application for Employment Authorization. Primary TPS regulations can be found at 8 C.F.R. § 244.

Caveat/Warnings

1. TPS does not lead the immigrant applicant to permanent resident status. However, during the time period in which a country or parts of a country have been designated for TPS, beneficiaries of TPS may remain in the United States and they may obtain work authorization.

2. When the Secretary of Homeland Security terminates a TPS designation, beneficiaries automatically revert to the same immigration status they had or maintained before their TPS (unless that previous status had since expired or been terminated), or they shift to any other status they may have acquired while registered for TPS.

3. In regards to 2 above, it is important to note that if an immigrant had unlawful or undocumented status prior to receiving TPS and did not obtain or acquire any lawful or documented status (other than TPS) during the TPS designation, he or she automatically reverts to that unlawful status upon the termination of that TPS designation.

Eligibility for TPS

An immigrant or alien who is a national of another country, or an immigrant or alien having no nationality (who last habitually resided in another country) designated for TPS is considered eligible to apply for TPS benefits if he or she satisfies the following:

(i) Establishes the necessary continuous physical presence and continuous residence in the United States as specified by each designation;

(ii) Is not subject to one of the criminal, security-related, or other bars to TPS; and

(iii) Timely applies for TPS benefits. If the Secretary of Homeland Security extends a TPS designation beyond the initial designation period, the beneficiary must timely register to maintain his or her TPS benefits under the TPS program.

An immigrant or alien is not eligible for TPS if he or she falls into the following categories:

An alien is not eligible for TPS if he or she:

(a) Has been convicted of any felony or two or more misdemeanors committed in the United States;

(b) Is a persecutor, or otherwise subject to one of the bars to asylum; or

(c) Is subject to one of several criminal-related or terrorism-related grounds of inadmissibility for which a waiver is not available.

[For more specific information relating to eligibility, see INA section 244(c)(2) and 8 CFR §§ 244.1 – 244.4.]

Some of the more-recently designated TPS countries include, among others:

Sierra Leone

Burundi

El Salvador

Honduras

Nicaragua

Somalia

Sudan, and

Liberia.

Liberia has also been recently designated a "Deferred Enforced Departure" (DED) country.

What is Deferred Enforced Department (DED)?

Deferred Enforced Department (DED) has been granted to nationals of certain countries by the President of the United States as an exercise of his or her constitutional power to conduct foreign relations. DED was apparently first used in 1990 and has been used about five times. In its past usage, DED has provided, among other things, temporary stay of removal and employment authorization for its beneficiaries.

[As previously stated in this book, the reader is specifically and particularly advised to consult a qualified immigration attorney or other qualified attorney for specific legal and immigration advice. Immigration law is a very serious, complex, and complicated subject.]

CHAPTER TWELVE:
The "Green Card" is Not Green

What is the "Green Card?"

The "Green Card," or Permanent Resident Card, serves as proof of an alien's lawful permanent resident status in the United States. A person with a Green Card has the right to live and work permanently in the United States. The Green Card also means that the individual is registered in the United States in accordance and compliance with United States immigration law.

The Green Card is a very valuable card. It gives the holder several rights, but <u>not</u> the right of citizenship nor all of the rights of a U.S. citizen. Green Card holders have several privileges, including:

(1) The right to live permanently in the United States;

(2) The right to work in the United States;

(3) The right to travel abroad for a certain period of time;

(4) The opportunity to apply for U.S. citizenship after a certain amount of years as a Green Card holder; and

(5) The right to petition for a Green Card for the applicant's spouse and any unmarried children under 21 years of age.

Green Cards were formerly issued by the Immigration and Naturalization Service (INS). That agency, which formerly was under the jurisdiction of the Attorney General of the United States and the U.S. Department of Justice, has since early 2003 been absorbed into and replaced by the Bureau of Citizenship and Immigration Services (BCIS). The BCIS is part of the new U.S. Department of Homeland Security (DHS). Shortly after the 2003 Homeland Security reorganization, BCIS was renamed to what is now U.S. Citizenship and Immigration Services (USCIS).

Privileges During "Green Card" Application

There are essentially two (2) important permits or privileges an alien can acquired while their Green Card application is pending:

(a) The first is a temporary work permit known as the Employment Authorization Document (EAD). This permit allows the person to be employed in the United States.

(b) The second is a temporary travel document, the so-called "advance parole," which allows the individual to "reenter" the United States. (Presumably, it is easier to get <u>out</u> of the United States than it is to get <u>in</u>.)

Both permits confer privileges and benefits that are independent to any existing status granted to the alien. As an example, it is possible that the alien may already have permission to work in the United States under an H1-B visa, which is a nonimmigrant classification used by an alien who will be employed temporarily in a specialty occupation.

The "Green Card" is not Green

Surprise! The "Green Card," or United States Permanent Resident Card, is not green. Further, the Green Card has not been "green" for a very long time. Since its inception in or about 1947, the card has taken on a variety of different colors at different times in history. The "Green Card" actually started out in about 1940 as a white card.

We probably still refer to these Permanent Resident Cards as "Green Cards" for historical reference reasons. For example, in the field of law we refer to intended distractions as "red herrings;" dismissal from employment notices are called "pink slips;" excessively sensationalized news stories are called "yellow journalism;" and the phrase "firing" or "to fire" someone when their job is terminated comes from the inspired practice of burning down the house of neighbors when they were no longer wanted in the community [Attorney Charles Jerome Ware, *Understanding The Law: A Primer*, 2008, iUniverse Press (1-800-288-4677), www.iuniverse.com, www.amazon.com]. In each of the above-referenced examples, an idea was originally associated with an actual item of the respective or specific color.

On the current, modern Green Card, created initially around 1995 or so, the pattern and color of the card changes continuously for security reasons. The information contained on the card includes, *inter alia,*

(1) the alien's name, (2) alien's number, (3) birth date, (4) issuing country (USA), (5) alien's country of birth, (6) immigrant case number, (7) "resident since" date, and (8) biometric data (fingerprint), *et al.*

It is important to note that, unlike American citizens when it comes to identification, U.S. permanent residents (Green Card holders) are required by law to carry their Green Cards with them (must be in their possession) *at all times.*

Ways To Obtain Permanent Resident Status

Generally, there are currently five (5) ways to get permanent resident status in the United States:

1. Permanent Residence through a family member;

2. Permanent Residence through employment;

3. Permanent Residence through investment;

4. Permanent Residence through the "Diversity Lottery;" and

5. Permanent Residence through "The Registry" provisions of the Immigration and Nationality Act.

[Source: USCIS, 2009]

PERMANENT RESIDENT ELIGIBILITY AND ESTIMATED QUOTAS

Category	Eligibility	Estimated Annual Quota	Approximate Alien Visa Backlog
Permanent Residence through a family member			
IR	Immediate relative (spouses, minor children and parents) of U.S. citizens. (A U.S. citizen must be at least 21 years of age in order to sponsor his or her parents).	No numerical limit	
F1	Unmarried sons and daughter (21 years of age or older) of U.S. citizens.	23,400	6-7 years
F2A	Spouses and minor children (under 21 years old) of lawful permanent residents.	87,934	5-6 years

Category	Eligibility	Estimated Annual Quota	Approximate Alien Visa Backlog
F2B	Unmarried sons and daughters (21 years of age or older) of lawful permanent residents.	26,266	9-10 years
F3	Married sons and daughters of U.S. citizens.	23,400	8-9 years
F4	Brothers and sisters of adult U.S. citizens.	65,000	10-11 years
Permanent Residence through employment			

Category	Eligibility	Estimated Annual Quota	Approximate Alien Visa Backlog
EB1	Priority workers. There are three subgroups: Foreign nationals with extraordinary ability in sciences, arts, education, business, or athletics OR Foreign nationals that are outstanding professors or researchers with at least three years of experience in teaching or research and who are recognized internationally, OR Foreign nationals that are managers and executives subject to international transfer to the United States.	40,000	Currently available

Category	Eligibility	Estimated Annual Quota	Approximate Alien Visa Backlog
EB2	Professionals holding advanced degrees (Ph.D., master's degree, or at least 5 years of progressive post-baccalaureate experience) or persons of exceptional ability in sciences, arts, or business.	40,000	Currently available
EB3	Skilled workers, professionals, and other workers.	40,000	5 years
EB4	Certain special immigrants – ministers, religious workers, current or former U.S. government workers, etc.	10,000	Currently available
EB5	Investors	10,000	Currently available
Diversity Immigrant (DV)		55,000	

Category	Eligibility	Estimated Annual Quota	Approximate Alien Visa Backlog
Political Asylum		No numerical limit	
Refugee		70,000	
IMPORTANT: Consult a qualified immigration lawyer for specific advice and consultation. Also, see USCIS and Visa bulletins and websites for up-to-date data. (2008)			

The Rest of the Story

And then there's the rest of the "Green Card" story....

What happens when a person "relinquishes" their Green Card? There are possible tax consequences, to start....

The Heroes Earnings Assistance and Relief Act of 2008 (The HEART Act)

The HEART Act, or so-called "apple pie" tax was intended and designed to help troops returning from war outside (of course) the U.S., veterans, and emergency workers. It imposes an exit tax that applies to expatriates and long-term U.S. Green Card-holding residents. The new law has been a bitter surprise to legal foreign workers and their multinational employers.

In compliance with the little-known HEART Act, foreign workers who have owned a Green Card for eight of the last 15 years, and choose to relinquish it, will be subject to federal taxation on unrealized income gains above $600,000. The Act applies to those individuals who have a federal tax liability greater than $139,000 a year, or have a net worth of more than $2 million, or have failed to certify to the IRS that they have been in compliance with United States federal tax obligations for the past five years [Daniel Sorid, "The (Tax) Law of Unintended Consequences," July 8, 2008; "Expatriate Rules in HEART," Deloitte].

If the holder does not relinquish his or her Green Card, they are subject to double taxation when living or working <u>outside</u> of the United States. This rule applies whether or not the person is living or working within their home country. Double taxation may be mitigated, however, by foreign tax credits.

On a scale of beef to pork, chicken to turkey…the HEART Act of 2008 is *sausage*.

CHAPTER THIRTEEN: The United States Immigration Judge

The Boss

In 1980, as a United States Immigration Judge I was assigned by President Jimmy Carter, Attorney General Griffin Bell, and Immigration and Naturalization Service (INS) Commissioner David Crosland to preside over several exclusions and deportation hearings everyday inside the old Atlanta Federal Penitentiary. This was part of the ongoing "Cuban (or Mariel) Boatlift Crisis."

There were three INS officers assigned to assist me in processing the hearings, and the other personnel around me were Federal Bureau of Prisons employees. Once we entered the prison in the morning, we could not leave until the end of the day for obvious security reasons. Our work days for the hearings lasted usually about twelve hours, and I rarely took time for lunch. During the designated lunch break of a half hour, I would usually sit at my desk (the Judge's Bench) and just meditate.

One day I was told that a new Bureau of Prisons employee had coincidentally walked by my hearing room, presumably on patrol of the prison, for a week at the same time I was meditating for a half hour or less.

"What does he do?," asked the new Bureau of Prisons employee of a fellow employee.

"To be honest, I don't know," replied the fellow employee. "All I know is that all of the INS employees call him the 'Boss.'"

All kidding aside, the United States Immigration Judge holds a very important position in this country's immigration practice, and in upholding America's immigration policies.

There are more than two hundred Immigration Judges currently located in more than fifty U.S. Immigration Courts throughout the country. They are part of the Office of the Chief Immigration Judge (OCIJ), which provides overall program direction, and articulates policies and procedures for immigration law enforcement. The OCIJ comes under the jurisdiction of the Executive Office for Immigration Review (EOIR), which is situated within the United States Department of Justice (DOJ), headed by the Attorney General of the United States. Got all that?

In their major function – removal proceedings – Immigration Judges determine after hearing and reviewing the evidence whether an individual from a foreign country (an alien) should be allowed to enter or to remain in the United States, or should be removed (also called "deported"). IJs are responsible for conducting formal court proceedings or hearings, and they are mandated to act independently in deciding the immigration issues and matters before them. Their decisions are administratively final in nature unless and until they are appealed or certified timely to the Board of Immigration Appeals (BIA).

IJs also have jurisdiction to consider various remedies or forms of relief from removal (or "deportation"). For example, in a typical removal proceeding, the Immigration Judge may decide whether an alien is removable (or "deportable") or inadmissible under the immigration laws. Then, the Judge may consider whether that alien may avoid removal by accepting voluntary departure or by qualifying for asylum, cancellation of removal ("deportation"), adjustment of status, protection under the United Nations Convention Against Torture, or other forms of relief.

As we know from my personal experience in the old Atlanta Federal Penitentiary in 1980 that I began this chapter with, many removal proceedings are conducted in prisons and jails. The name given currently for the initiative is the Criminal Alien Program. The Program involves coordination with the Department of Homeland Security (DHS) and correctional authorities in all fifty states, Puerto Rico, the District of Columbia, selected municipalities, the Federal Bureau of Prisons, and other law enforcement entities.

Immigration Judges conduct on-site hearings to adjudicate the immigration status of alien inmates while they are serving sentences for criminal convictions.

Asylum and the Immigration Court

Recently the United Nations reported that in the year 2005 there were more than 190 million international migrants throughout the world. This was about 3% of the world's population. Not all of these aliens are seeking to enter the United States. Aliens on the move who have departed their home countries to move elsewhere are a worldwide phenomenon [*TRAC Immigration Report*, http://trac.syr.edu/immigration/reports/161/].

The Immigration Judge is frequently crucial in the asylum-seeking process in the United States. Though certainly <u>not</u> all asylum seekers want to immigrate to the U.S., tens of thousands each year do in fact seek asylum here. Under the authority of well-established United Nations conventions and American immigration law, many of these asylum requests are processed by the Immigration Court. It is reported that during the past decade or so, these IJs have decided on the merits approximately 35,000 or so asylum requests each year. Considering the ongoing controversy over immigration in this country, one would reasonably expect that this figure would be higher.

For the asylum-seeking cases it receives by way of its original jurisdiction through the Executive Office of Immigration Review (EOIR) as well as from USCIS (United States Citizenship and Immigration Services), the Immigration Court is a critical decision maker in this complex and complicated mixture of human dynamics, American immigration law, and international treaties or conventions. It is a crucial moment in each and every asylum hearing when the Immigration Judge, after considering all of the evidence, makes the decision to (1) *deny* the asylum application, and thus presenting the normal probability of removal or deportation, or (2) *grant* the asylum on either an absolute or conditional basis.

Asylum Seekers by Nationality

Individuals seeking asylum in the United States before the Immigration Court come from many countries. For several years, Chinese asylum seekers have made up the largest group of cases decided by the Court. Chinese asylum seekers represent over one in five (or 22.3%) of every asylum seeker since the year 2000. During the same period of time, Haitian and Columbian asylum seekers represented 9.3% (one in eleven) and 9.1%, respectively. Other countries in the top asylum-seeker ranks include, *inter alia*, Albania, India, and El Salvador.

Obviously considering the mandated legal and factual grounds for successful asylum claims, applicants for asylum from some countries tend to be more successful than others. Since the year 2000, more than 80 percent of asylum seekers from El Salvador, Mexico and Haiti, for instances, have been *denied* asylum. At the other extreme of the spectrum, though less plentiful, asylum applicants from Afghanistan and Burma have a 70 percent chance of having their asylum applications *granted*.

Importance of Legal Representation

Get a qualified immigration lawyer.

When an applicant has to appear before an IJ, it is very helpful to have representation by a qualified immigration lawyer. The data is in, and it is clear, about this point.

The data indicates clearly that an important determining factor in the decision-making process before an Immigration Judge is the presence or absence of legal representation for the asylum seeker. About 64% of asylum applications with legal representation are *denied* by IJs, so having a lawyer certainly does not automatically guarantee success. However, the asylum *denial* rate for those persons without legal representation is a whopping 93%!

Requests for Asylum in the United States (USCIS and EOIR)	Number of Requests	Percent Denied
All asylum seekers (including USCIS and EOIR)	297,240	69.0%
Without Attorney (EOIR)	51,254	93.4%
With Attorney (EOIR)	245,982	64.0%
Approx. Time Period: 2000-2005 Source: http://trac.syr.edu/immigration/reports/160		

CHAPTER FOURTEEN: The United States Citizen and Immigration Service (USCIS)

After the "9/11" (2001) terrorist attacks on the United States, attitudes about immigrants in many quarters of the country changed. The Homeland Security Act of 2002 was enacted and the U.S. Department of Homeland Security was created. This new department includes the new U.S. Citizen and Immigration Service (USCIS), which includes many functions of my old employer, the U.S. Immigration and Naturalization Service (INS). The new change in attitude about immigrants has not been as severe as that of the parrot, however:

Changed Attitude

Omar received a parrot for his birthday. This parrot was fully grown with a very bad attitude and an even more atrocious vocabulary. Every other word out of the parrot's mouth was an expletive worthy of deletion. Those words that were not expletives were, to put it mildly, quite rude.

Omar tried diligently to change the caustic bird's attitude and he consistently used polite words around the bird, played soft and melodic music and did other polite, courteous and gentile things around the crude bird. Alas...nothing worked. Finally, in frustration, Omar yelled at the bird; but the parrot got even worse. In a fit of violence he shook the parrot, but the bird got even more angry and a lot more rude.

Finally...ultimately, Omar inserted the outrageously rude and crude bird into the kitchen freezer. For a few moments he listened and heard the parrot squawking, kicking, and screaming like crazy. Then suddenly things got very quiet in the freezer. Ominously quiet.

Suddenly, too, Omar became frightened that he might have actually injured or even killed the bird, so he quickly opened the freezer door to check on it.

The prideful but obviously shaken parrot calmly stepped forward, out of the freezer, onto the extended arm of Omar and said: "I am sorry that I offended you with my crude language and rude actions. I respectfully ask for your forgiveness. I will certainly try diligently to check my actions and improve my behavior as well as my language."

Omar was absolutely astounded by what appeared to be a genuine change of improvement in the parrot's attitude, demeanor and language. He was just getting ready to ask the bird "what" had changed him or "why" he had changed his negative attitude when the parrot continued,

"May I ask what the chicken [in the freezer] did to deserve his fate?"

USCIS

The USCIS is a department within the monstrous and new U.S. Department of Homeland Security (DHS). USCIS was created by the Homeland Security Act of 2002, and replaced the U.S. Immigration and Naturalization Service (INS). The USCIS consists of approximately 15,000 to 20,000 employees and at least 250 to 300 field offices around the world. The internal goal of the USCIS, in terms of its budget, is to acquire the bulk of its funding from processing fees that are required from applicants when processing the forms and petitions it receives. The USCIS includes the Office of Citizenship, which is within the Department of Homeland Security. This branch of the USCIS disseminates information about the responsibilities of U.S. citizenship and educational materials relating to U.S. history and civic culture.

Mission of the USCIS

The stated mission of the USCIS includes:

(i) promotion of U.S. national security;

(ii) improvement in "customer" service;

(iii) avoidance of backlogs of immigration cases; and

(iv) working towards development of solutions to immigration problems that are brought to the USCIS's attention by the public, special interest groups, government agencies, and the Congress.

Functions of the USCIS

The USCIS has the following declared functions:

(1) Adjudications of immigrant visa petitions;

(2) Adjudications of naturalization petitions;

(3) Administration of immigration services and benefits;

(4) Adjudications of asylum and refugee claims;

(5) Issuing employment authorization documents (EAD);

(6) Adjudications of petitions for nonimmigrant temporary workers (H-1B, O-1, etc);

(7) Granting lawful permanent resident status; and

(8) Granting citizenship.

The USCIS also handles all other adjudications performed by the former INS, including the adjudications performed at USCIS service centers. USCIS oversees the programs that administer immigrant service benefits such as foreign student authorization, asylum and refugee status, inter-country adoptions, family and employment-related immigration, employment authorization, and the replacement of immigration documents. The USCIS does not handle immigration enforcement, which is carried out by U.S. Immigration and Customs Enforcement (ICE).

Executive Office for Immigration Review (EOIR)

The EOIR is where the United States Immigration Judges (IJs) and the Board of Immigration Appeals (BIA), among others, are located. As an office within the United States Department of Justice, EOIR is headquartered in Falls Church, Virginia.

EOIR's key mission is to adjudicate (using immigration judges and other professionals) immigration cases. These cases include, among others, cases involving detained aliens, alleged criminal aliens, and aliens seeking asylum as a form of relief from exclusion and removal (or deportation) from the United States.

CHAPTER FIFTEEN:
Fundamentals of Immigration and Naturalization Law

What do you call a hundred white guys chasing a Black guy of mixed race descent?
Answer: The PGA (Professional Golf Association).

"They say there are something like 12 million illegal immigrants in the country right now, with another half a million coming every year. Remember in the last election when the Democrats claimed there was two Americas? Turns out one of them was Mexico." – Jay Leno, TV Show Host and Comedian.

"The liberals are saying that this guest worker program…is really just a way to depress wages and create a permanent underclass of exploited labor. To which the president Bush said, 'And the problem is?'" – Bill Maher, TV Host and Comedian.

There are four (4) major and fundamental principles which have, for many years, been the foundation underlying United States policy on legal permanent immigration. These four principles are:

(i) the reunification of families;

(ii) the admission of immigrants with needed skills;

(iii) the protection of refugees; and

(iv) the diversity of admissions by the country of origin.

These fundamental principles are embodied in Federal immigration law, such as the Immigration and Nationality Act (INA) which was first codified in 1952, and in the various relevant United Nations treaties and/ or conventions. The U.S. Congress has significantly modified and amended the INA several times since 1952. For instance, in 2002 Congress amended the INA with enactment of the Enhanced Border Security and Visa Reform Act of 2002 (P.L. 107-173).

Previous major laws which amended the INA include:

(1) the Immigration Amendments of 1965;

(2) the Refugee Act of 1980;

(3) the Immigration Reform and Control Act of 1986;

(4) the Immigration Act of 1990; and

(5) The Illegal Immigration Reform and Immigrant Responsibility Act of 1996.

[CRS Report for Congress, the Library of Congress, Order Code RS20919, "Immigration and Naturalization Fundamentals," by Ruth Ellen Wasem, Updated May 20, 2003].

Aliens, Immigrants and Nonimmigrants

An "alien" is legally defined as any person not a citizen or national of the United States. An "alien" is synonymous with a "noncitizen." Aliens include individuals who are here in the United States legally, as well as people who are here in violation of the INA. The term "noncitizen" is generally used to describe all foreign-born persons in the United States who have not been citizens.

There are two essential types of categories of "legal aliens": immigrants and nonimmigrants. Technically, immigrants are individuals who are admitted as legal permanent residents (LPRs) of the United States. "Nonimmigrants," on the other hand, such as tourists, foreign students, diplomats, temporary agricultural workers, exchange visitors, or intracompany business personnel, are admitted for a specific purpose and a temporary period of time. Nonimmigrants are required to leave the country when their visas expire, though certain classes of nonimmigrants may adjust to LPR status if they otherwise qualify.

Nonimmigrants are frequently referred to by the letter that denotes this section in the INA statute, such as H-2A for agricultural workers, F-1 for foreign students, or J-1 for cultural exchange visitors.

Because immigrants hold a more favored status in this country over nonimmigrants, the requirements for the admission of immigrants are much more strict or stringent than for nonimmigrants. Far fewer immigrants than nonimmigrants are admitted each year. Once they are admitted, immigrants may accept and change employment, and may apply for United States citizenship through the *naturalization* process. Generally after five (5) years of continuous residency.

Immigration "Preference" Categories and Numerical Limits

Historically, there are controversial subjects within the field of immigration and naturalization.

In theory, though frequently not in practice, American immigration admissions are subject to a complex set of numerical limits and preference categories that give priority for admissions to this country on the basis of (i) family relationships, (ii) needed skills for the nation, and (iii) a geographic diversity. In the year 2003, for example, American immigration admissions included a (i) *flexible worldwide cap of 675,000 admissions*, not including asylees and refugees, and (b) a *per-country of origin ceiling*, which changes yearly.

In 2003, immigration admissions allocated to the *three (3) preference tracks* included:

(i) 226,000 minimum on the basis of family relations;

(ii) 140,000 limit for needed skills (employment-based admissions); and

(iii) 55,000 for geographic diversity immigrant admissions. This last category was based on a formula-generated visa lottery allegedly aimed at countries that have low levels of immigration to the United States.

Immigration Loop-Holes

A major loop-hole in these limits comes into play when one learns that the so-called "per-country ceilings" for immigrant admissions may be exceeded for the "needed skills" (employment-based) immigrants, even though the worldwide limit (in 2003) of 140,000 employment-based admissions ostensibly remains in effect.

Additionally, "immediate relatives of U.S. citizens" are admitted even if their numbers are above the numerical limits of the "per-country ceilings," and are the "flexible" component of the worldwide cap. Immediate relatives of U.S. citizens include their spouses, unmarried minor children, and the parents of adult U.S. citizens.

2001 Immigrant Admissions by Category	
A. Immediate relatives of U.S. Citizens (Family-Based)	443,964
B. Family preference immigrants (Family-Based)	232,143
C. Employment preference (Needed Skills)	179,195
D. Refugee and Asylee Adjustments	108,506
E. Geographic Diversity	42,506
F. Other (including among others, 18,926 Nicaraguans)*	58,495
TOTAL:	1,064,318

SOURCE: Congressional Research Service, The Library of Congress, CRS Report for Congress, "Immigration and Naturalization Fundamentals," by Ruth Ellen Wasem, May 20, 2003.

* Note: The largest group in the "other" category are the 18,926 Nicaraguans who adjusted to Legal Permanent Resident (LPR) status through special legislation, i.e., the Nicaraguan and Central American Relief Act of 1997.]

The Naturalization Process

The "naturalization" process is another tradition of immigration policy designed to integrate immigrants fully into American society.

Under long-standing U.S. immigration law all legal permanent residents (LPRs) are "potential" citizens of the United States and may become citizens through this process known as "naturalization." To *naturalize*, aliens:

(i) Must have continuously lived in the United States for 5 years as LPRs (in the case of spouses of U.S. citizens, 3 years residence is enough);

(ii) demonstrate that they have good moral character;

(iii) demonstrate the ability to read, write, speak, and understand English;

(iv) pass an examination on U.S. government and history;

(v) pay the required fees of at least $310 when they file their applicant materials; and

(vi) choose the option of either taking a standardized civics test or of having the examiner quiz them on civics as part of their interview.

Immigration Loop-Holes (Exceptions)

Generally, the English language requirement is waived for those individuals who are at least 50 years old and have lived in the United States at least 20 years, or who are at least 55 years old and have lived in the United States at least 15 years. So-called "special consideration" can be given on the civics requirement if the alien applicant is over 65 years old and has lived in the United States for at least 20 years.

Further, both the civics and the English language requirements are waived for those applicants who are unable to comply because of physical or development disabilities or mental impairment. Other loop-holes or waivers can be had for those applicants who have served in the U.S. military.

The most recent highs in petitions for naturalization (to become American citizens) came in the mid-1990s when over a million people annually sough naturalization [Source: CRS; Bureau of Citizenship and Immigration Services data; 2003].

Paying Taxes

Aliens in the United States are generally subject to the same tax obligations, including Social Security (FICA) and unemployment (FUTA) as citizens of the United States, with the exception of certain nonimmigrant students and cultural exchange visitors. LPRs are treated the same as citizens for tax purposes. Other aliens, including unauthorized migrants, are held to a "substantive presence" test based upon the number of days they have been in the United States. Some countries have reciprocal tax treaties with the United States that – depending on the terms of the particular treaty – exempt citizens of their country living in the United States from certain taxes in the United States.

Exclusion and Removal (Deportation) from the United States

Exclusion and removal (deportation) proceedings, along with asylum hearings, are major staples for the United States Immigration Judge and the EOIR of the Department of Justice.

Generally speaking, all aliens to the United States must satisfy State Department consular officers abroad and the Department of Homeland Security (DHS) Bureau of Customs and Border Protection inspectors upon entry to the U.S. that they (the aliens) are not ineligible for visas or admission under the so-called "grounds of inadmissibility" of the Immigration and Nationality Act (INA).

Officially, the nine (9) INA "grounds of inadmissibility" are:

(1) health-related grounds

(2) criminal history;

(3) national security and terrorist concerns;

(4) public charge (e.g., indigence);

(5) seeking to work without proper labor certification;

(6) illegal entrants and immigration law violations;

(7) lacking proper documents;

(8) ineligible for citizenship; and, of course,

(9) aliens previously removed.

Of course, there are exceptions. Some categories may be waived or are not applicable in the case of nonimmigrants, refugees (e.g., on the theory, for example, of public charge), and other aliens. By the way, under new rules all family-based immigrants entering the United States after December 18, 1997, are required to have a new binding affidavit of support signed by the U.S. sponsor (under oath) in order to meet the "public charge" requirement.

The INA goes further and details the specific circumstances and actions in several cases that can result in aliens being deported (removed) from the United States. "Criminal" grounds for removal have been of special concern in recent years. The Illegal Immigration Reform and Immigrant Responsibility Act of 1996 (IIRIRA) expanded and toughened the deportation consequences of criminal convictions, and further made the consequences *retroactive*.[1] In addition, the category of "terrorist" grounds have been enlarged and tightened, made more strict by the U.S.A. Patriot Act of 2001 (P.O. 107-77).

---

1   The retroactive provision was subsequently overturned by the U.S. Supreme Court in 2001.

As usual, we caution the reader specifically and particularly to seek legal advice and consultation with a competent immigration professional for specific questions.

CHAPTER SIXTEEN: What is an "Illegal Alien," exactly?

Tasteless Joke of the Day

Is it just me or does anyone else find this amazing when it comes to the "Mad Cow" disease problem? Our Federal government can track down a cow born in Canada almost three years ago, right to the exact stall where the cow sleeps in the state of Washington. Our government can also track that cow's calves to their exact stalls. But, our government is unable to locate 12 million illegal aliens wandering around our country!

The solution appears to be to give every alien a cow.

A tasteless, uninformed joke. And not terribly funny. The problem is that there are a lot of people out there who are similarly uninformed about how the process works.

In America, no human being is "illegal."

First of all, under United States immigration law there is *no* such legal term as "illegal alien." In United States laws, an "alien" is a legal term for a person or individual either a human being or a corporation (business), who is not a United States national [Source: definition, U.S. Citizenship and Immigration Services, *et al.*]. The Federal government's use of the legal term "alien" dates back to 1798, when the famous Alien and Sedition Acts defined "aliens" as potential enemies of the state [INA, 8 USC 1101[1]; "Key Terms in Latino/A Cultural and Literary Studies," by Paul Allatson (2006), Blackwell Publishing].

Colloquially, so-called "illegal aliens" or "unauthorized aliens" are identified by some as being those noncitizens who either entered the United States surreptitiously or who overstayed the term of their nonimmigrant visas. The "surreptitious" entries are usually considered those aliens who entered without inspection (so-called EWI), and the "overstayed their visa" (OTVs) entries are usually tourists or students.

I prefer to call them "undocumented" aliens, particularly since in America no human being is "illegal."

Actually, many of these "undocumented" or "unauthorized" aliens have some type of documentation, though probably either bogus or expired. Many actually have cases pending with the Bureau of Citizenship and Immigration Service (BCIS). The former Immigration and Naturalization Service (INA) estimated that there were 7.0 million "unauthorized aliens" in the United States in 2000. Current and various reports today (2009) place these estimates between 12 and 20 million "unauthorized aliens."

Eligibility for Federal Benefits

So-called "noncitizens'" or "unauthorized aliens'" eligibility for major federal benefit programs depend on their immigration status and whether they arrived before or after enactment of P.L. 104-193, the 1996 welfare law (as amended by P.L. 105-33 and P.L. 105-185). Refugees remain eligible for Supplemental Security Income (SSI) and Medicare for 7 years after arrival, and for other restricted programs for 5 years. Most LPRs are barred SSI until they naturalize or meet a 10-year work requirement. LPRs receiving SSI (and SSI-related Medicaid) on August 22, 1996, the enactment date of P.L. 104-193, continue to be eligible, as do those here then whose subsequent disability makes them eligible for SSI and Medicaid. All LPRs who meet a 5-year residence test and all LPR children (regardless of date of entry or length of residence) are eligible for food stamps. LPRs entering after August 22, 1996, are barred from Temporary assistance for Needy Families (TANF) and Medicaid for 5 years, after which their coverage becomes a state option. Also after the 5-year bar, the sponsor's income is deemed to be available to new immigrants in determining their financial eligibility for designated federal means-tested programs until they naturalize or meet the work requirement. Unauthorized aliens, i.e., undocumented aliens, are ineligible for almost all federal benefits except, for example, emergency medical care [CRS Report RL31114, *Noncitizen Eligibility for Major Federal Public Assistance Programs: Policies and Legislation*, by Ruth Ellen Wasem and Joe Richardson].

In sum, in America no human being is "illegal."

CHAPTER SEVENTEEN:
A Summary of Immigration
Law in the United States

Late Night Immigration Humor

"Don't blame illegal immigrants for driving down wages. Blame Congress. Republicans in Congress have to stop saying that the problem with Mexicans coming over the board is they keep wages down. You know what keeps wages down? The fact that Congress hasn't raised the minimum wage since 1997. 1997, when my dealer still had a beeper! Car dealer, car dealer, what did I say?" – From Comedian Bill Maher's "New Rules."

The Senate has passed a resolution to make English the official language of the United States. Today President Bush said this is the 'goodest news' he's heard in a long time." – Jay Leno

As previously stated in this book, the U.S. Congress has complete authority over American immigration. Presidential power generally does not extend beyond refugee policy, such as the 1980 Cuban (Mariel) Boatlift Crisis, the Haitian Refugee Crisis of the 1980s and 1990s, and so forth. With the exception of questions concerning aliens' constitutional rights, the U.S. courts have generally concluded the immigration issue to be nonjusticiable, i.e., not capable of being decided on the merits in a court of law and/or equity.

The stated overall purpose of Federal immigration law is to determine whether a person is an alien; that individual's rights, duties, and responsibilities associated with being an alien in the United States; and how that alien gains residence or citizenship within the United States. Further, Federal immigration law provides the process by which certain eligible aliens can become legally "naturalized" citizens with full rights of citizenship. Immigration law serves as a gatekeeper for the country's borders, deciding who may enter, how long they may stay in this country, and when they must depart from our nation [Legal Information Institute, Cornell University Law School, 2008; http://topics.law.cornell.edu/wex/immigration].

To the extent that individual states within the United States have power concerning immigration issues, their power is severely limited. Federal law 28 U.S.C. § 1251 specifies with particularity the complete extent of state immigration jurisdiction. Another statute, 28 U.S.C. § 994, presents the Federal sentencing guidelines for unlawful entry into the United States.

In theory, though not in practice, the Federal government believes it can achieve its goals of immigration control by controlling the visa process. It has not worked, generally,

There are effectively two types of U.S. visas: (1) the immigrant visa, and (2) the nonimmigrant visa.

Immigrant visas allow the holders to stay in the U.S. permanently and eventually to apply for citizenship (become "naturalized"). Aliens with immigrant visas also can work in the United States. Congress limits the number of immigrant visas each year, and several immigrant visas are subject to per-country caps [See Chapters 12 and 15, *supra*]. Over the past couple of decades or so, 675,000 immigrant visas have tended to be Congress' favorite limit per year.

Nonimmigrant visas are primarily issued to tourists and temporary business visitors. These nonimmigrant visas are typically sorted by the Federal government into eighteen (18) different types. Many of these nonimmigrant visa types are not subject to caps on their numbers that may be granted in a year. However, there are only a few categories of nonimmigrant visas that allow their holders to work in the United States.

History of American Immigration Law

Historically, it appears that the first documented attempt by the U.S. Congress to set immigration policy came in or about 1790 with the enactment of the "Naturalization Act of 1790." This Act restricted naturalization to **"free white persons"** of "good moral character." It also required the **"white"** applicant for naturalization or citizenship to have lived in the country for two years prior to becoming naturalized.

In 1795 Congress amended the Naturalization Act of 1790 and increased the residency requirement for **"free white persons…of good moral character"** to five (5) years. This five (5) year residency requirement for naturalized citizenship for *all* applicants remains the law to this very day.

Upon final ratification of the Fourteenth Amendment to the United States Constitution, July 9, 1868, all children born within the United States received citizenship. That law is in effect to this very day.

Finally, in 1870, Congress broadened the process of "naturalization" to permit African-Americans the right to become naturalized citizens.

Reacting to widespread xenophobia (fear and hatred of strangers or foreigners, or anything that is strange or foreign) from an influx of Asian aliens between about 1850 and 1882, Congress passed into law the Chinese Exclusion Act of 1882. The Act, signed by President Chester A. Arthur after being passed by Congress, provided an absolute 10-year moratorium on Chinese labor immigration. This Act was the first time Federal law denied entry of an ethnic working group on the basis that it endangered the "good order" of certain localities within the United States.

The 1921 Emergency Quota Act

Moving forward to the twentieth century, in 1921 Congress passed the Emergency Immigration Act, creating national immigration quotas. It was also known as the Emergency Quota Act, and as the Johnson Quota Act. The law limited the annual number of immigrants who could be admitted from any country to 3% of the number of persons from that country living in the United States in 1910, according to the U.S. Census data. This totaled about 357,802 immigrants. Of that 357,802 immigrants, just over a half of them were allocated for northern and western Europeans, and the balance was reserved for eastern and southern Europeans (a 75% drop from previous years). So-called "professionals" were permitted in from these areas despite their origins. They were, of course, all "white" or Anglo-Saxon.

On average, the annual influx of immigrants prior to 1921 was 176,983 from northern and western Europe, and 685,531 from other countries primarily southern and eastern Europe. The 1921 Emergency Quota Act set no limits on immigration from Latin America.

The Immigration Act of 1924

The Immigration Act of 1925, or the so-called Johnson-Reed Act, which included the National Origins Act and the Asian Exclusion Act, succeeded and superseded the 1921 Emergency Quota Act. This Federal law reduced the annual quota of immigrants from 3% down to 2% of the number of persons from the applicable country living in the United States in 1890 (*not* 1910), according to the U.S. Census figures for 1890. The Act excluded immigration of Asians altogether, and the combined number of immigrants from the eastern hemisphere could not eclipse 154,227 immigrants.

This Act is credited with being the first *permanent* limitation on immigration into the United States, and is said to have established the "national origins quota system." In coordination and conjunction with the 1917 Immigration Act, the Immigration Act of 1924 (the National Origins Quota Act), controlled and guided immigration policy in the United States until the enactment of the Immigration and Nationality Act of 1952.

But before we discuss the Immigration and Nationality Act of 1952 (INA), and move into the area of "modern immigration law," a quick discussion of the 1917 Immigration Act would be in order.

The 1917 Immigration Act

Though infrequently mentioned and discussed in American immigration lore, the Immigration Act of 1917, also known as the "Asiatic Barred Zone Act" is actually quite famous, or infamous as the case may be. It was initially vetoed by President Woodrow Wilson on December 14, 1916, as it should have been; but it was subsequently passed on February 4, 1917 with an overwhelming majority vote of the United States Congress.

The 1917 Immigration Act contributed considerable provocative, contentious, and controversial language to American immigration law, policy, and practice. For example, the Act:

(i) increased the entry head tax for immigrants to $8 (a lot of money in 1917);

(ii) added the following persons to the list of "excluded" and "excludable" immigrants from the United States:

"all idiots, imbeciles, feeble-minded persons, epileptics, insane persons; persons who have had one or more attacks of insanity at any time previously; persons of constitutional psychopathic inferiority; persons with chronic alcoholism; paupers; professional beggars; vagrants; persons afflicted with tuberculosis in any form or with a loathsome or dangerous contagious disease; persons not comprehended within any of the foregoing excluded cases who are found to be and are certified by the examining surgeon as being mentally or physically defective, such physical defect being of a nature which may affect the ability of such alien to earn a living; persons who have been convicted of or admit having committed a felony or other crime or misdemeanor involving moral turpitude; polygamists, or persons who practice polygamy, or being in or advocate the practice of polygamy; anarchists, or persons who believe in or advocate the overthrow by force or violence of the Government of the United States;"

(iii) and a highly controversial proposal of the Act was to exclude all –

"aliens over sixteen years of age, physically capable of reading, who cannot read the English language, or some other language or dialect, including Hebrew or Yiddish." Attempts at introducing literacy tests had been vetoed by Grover Cleveland in 1891 and William Taft in 1913. President Woodrow Wilson also objected to this clause in the 1917 Immigration Act but it was still passed by Congress,

(iv) Another incendiary aspect of the 1917 Act was the section of the law that designated a so-called "Asiatic Barred Zone." This "zone" was a geographic region that included much of eastern Asia and the Pacific Islands from which persons could not immigrate into the United States. Previously, as we now know from discussing the Chinese Exclusion Act 1882, *et al.*, only the Chinese had been excluded from admission as immigrants to America, *supra*. The 1917 Act reflected America's renewed nativist and xenophobic sentiments about Asians, particularly China and Japan.

Despite the monstrous immigration issues and problems raised by the 1917 Immigration Act, the 1924 Immigration Act was considered to be even more restrictive and onerous ["Learning Curve," The National Archives, 01/12/2009; http://www.spartacus.schoolnet. co.uk/USAE1917A.htm].

The Immigration and Nationality Act of 1952 (INA), also known as "The McCarran-Walter Act of 1952"

It should be understood that it is the "Immigration Act of 1917 (or Asiatic Barred Zone Act)" that was later amended and put into the Immigration and Nationality Act of 1952 (INA) (or "McCarran-Walter Act of 1952"). Not as many people think, the "Immigration Act of 1924."

In other words, the Immigration Act of 1917 is the forerunner of the INA of 1952.

The INA of 1952 ("McCarran-Walter Act") extended the privilege of naturalization to Japanese, Koreans, and other Asians, and in the process amended and adopted other aspects of the Immigration Act of 1917 ("Asiatic Barred Zone Act") [see, "Commentary on Excerpt of the McCarran-Walter Act, 1952," *American Journal Online: The Immigrant Experience*, Primary Source Microfilm (1999), History Resource Center, Farmington Hills, Michigan, Gale Group, February 9, 2007]. The INA of 1952 revised and amended all previous laws and regulations regarding immigration, naturalization, and nationality, and brought them all together into one comprehensive (and allegedly cohesive) statute ["McCarran-Walter Act," *Dictionary of American History*, 7 volumes, Charles Scribner's Sons, (1976), Reproduced in History Resource Center, Farmington Hills, Michigan: Gale Group, February 9, 2007].

In sum, in order to better understand the Immigration and Nationality Act of 1952 (INA), one should study the Immigration Act of 1917 for legislative history purposes, at the very least.

The INA, among other things, eliminated *all* race-based quotas, replacing these quotas with purely nationality-based quotas, to this very day, even in this "Post 9/11/2001" environment – and the new Homeland Security Act of 2002, the INA continues to strongly influence the field of American immigration law.

To enforce the Congressionally-mandated quotas, the INA created the Immigration and Naturalization Service (INS). The INS served at the point for the remainder of the 20th century as the Federal agency charged with enforcing these quotas. The agency operated under the jurisdiction of the U.S. Department of Justice and the Attorney General of the United States until the creation and opening of the U.S. Department of Homeland Security on March 1, 2003 [see Chapters 12, 13, 14, 15 and 16, *supra*].

The Immigration Reform and Control Act of 1986

A perceived need to curtail or halt "illegal immigration" moved Congress to enact a new law in 1986: the Immigration Reform and Control Act (IRCA) of 1986, also known as the "Simpson-Mazzoli Act." This Act was signed into law by President Ronald Reagan on November 6, 1986.

In a nutshell (pardon the pun), the Act toughened criminal sanctions against employers who hired "illegal aliens," denied "illegal aliens" federally-funded welfare, and it legitimized some aliens through an amnesty program [see, Chapter 16: "What is an 'Illegal Alien', exactly?," *supra*].

The Immigration Marriage Fraud Amendments of 1986

The "Immigration Marriage Fraud Amendments of 1986," or Public Law 99-639, was passed into law by Congress on November 10, 1986 – four days after the Immigration Reform and Control Act of 1986. The law's stated purpose was to deter or stop immigration-related marriage fraud or so-called "sham marriages."

A major provision of the law stipulates that aliens who derive their immigrant status based upon a "marriage" of less than two years duration are "conditional" immigrants. In order to remove their "conditional" status these immigrants must apply at a U.S. Citizenship and Immigration Services office during the 90-day period before their second anniversary of receiving conditional status. If the aliens cannot demonstrate to USCIS that the marriage through which the conditional status was obtained was and is in fact a valid marriage, their conditional immigrant status may be terminated and they may be removable or deportable [Source: USCIS].

The Immigration Act of 1990

The Immigration Act of 1990 is most well-known for the lottery program it created that randomly assigned a number of visas to immigrants. In sum, the Act increased the number of "legal" immigrants allowed into the United States each year. The alleged goal of the lottery was to help immigrants enter the United States from Countries where the U.S. did not often grant immigrant visas. The laws also provided exceptions for the English testing process required for naturalization set out in the old Naturalization Act of 1906.

Before the Act was passed on November 29, 1990, about 500,000 new immigrants annually were admitted to the U.S. for several years. After the Act was passed, that number rose to over 700,000 annually.

In addition to the foregoing, the Immigration Act of 1990 revised the grounds for exclusion and deportation, authorized temporary protected status (see Chapter 11, *supra*), to aliens of designated countries, revised and established new nonimmigrant admission categories, revised and extended the Visa Waiver Pilot Program, and revised naturalization authority and requirements.

The Act further strengthened the U.S. Border Patrol, and it amended certain language concerning disease restrictions under the INA in such a way that permitted the Secretary of Health and Human Services (HHS) to remove the disease AIDS from the list of illnesses making a prospective immigrant normally ineligible to enter the country.

The Illegal Immigration Reform and Immigrant Responsibility Act (IIRIRA) of 1996

As a lawyer and as a former U.S. Immigration Judge, I have never cared much for the IIRIRA of 1996.

First of all, the name of this Act is entirely too long and convoluted. Who are you trying to impress, Congress?

We frequently call this Act "IRA-IRA" for short. It is not an intelligent law, and it has dramatically changed the immigration laws here in the United States [see, Chapter 15, *supra*].

Before "IRA-IRA," aliens were subject to immediate deportation or removal only for criminal offenses that could lead the person to five years or more incarceration. Now, under "IRA-IRA," minor or misdemeanor offenses could make an individual alien eligible for removal/deportation. The Act applies even to immigrants who have married American citizens, and even though they may have sired American-born children.

When the Illegal Immigration Reform and Immigrant Responsibility Act of 1996 (IIRIRA), or "IRA-IRA" was passed by Congress in 1996, it was applied retroactively to all those convicted of deportable offenses. This included U.S. residents who committed minor offenses decades ago. However, in 2001, the U.S. Supreme Court decided that Congress did not intend IIRIRA to be applied retroactively to those who pleaded guilty to a crime prior to the enactment of IIRIRA, if that person would not have been deportable at the time that he pleaded guilty [INS v. St. Cyr, (00-767), 533 U.S. 289 (2001), 229 F.3d 406, affirmed]. In spite of the 2001 ruling the way the IIRIRA law is used in practice has had so little public scrutiny and oversight so as to make its further use questionable.

In an effort to curb "illegal immigration," Congress voted to double the U.S. Border Patrol to 10,000 agents over five years and mandated the construction of fences at the most heavily trafficked areas of the U.S.-Mexico border. Congress also approved a pilot program to check the immigration status of job applicants; which, actually, appears to help somewhat.

IIRIRA's mandatory detention provisions have also been repeatedly challenged, with less success.

In my opinion "IRA-IRA" was, and is, bad immigration law – from start to finish.

CHAPTER EIGHTEEN:
American Immigration in the "Post – 9/11/2001" Environment

"People who love sausage and respect the law should never watch either one being made."

– *"Attorney's Note," page 2*
Understanding The Law: A Primer, by Attorney Charles Jerome Ware, iUniverse Press *(2008), www.amazon.com (Books).*

After the September 11, 2001 terrorist attacks on the United States, the Bush Administration and Congress set out to change the Federal government bureaucracy. The results included, among other legislative and administrative changes, the controversial "USA Patriot Act (2001)" and the "Homeland Security Act of 2002." Both laws are in fact "sausage" legislation, proverbially.

Homeland Security Act of 2002

The Homeland Security Act of 2002 created the U.S. Department of Homeland Security on March 1, 2003, replacing the Immigration and Naturalization Service (INS) which had been in existence technically since June 22, 1870 (for about 133 years). INS superseded the previous immigration agency, Immigration and Customs Enforcement.

The vast majority of INS's duties and responsibilities were transferred to three (3) new agencies within the Department of Homeland Security (DHS):

(i) the administration of immigration services, including permanent residence, naturalization, asylum, and other functions became the responsibility of the Bureau of Citizenship and Immigration Services (BCIS) of DHS; which actually existed as BCIS for only a brief period of time before changing its name to the United States Citizenship and Immigration Services (USCIS);

(ii) the INS's investigative and enforcement functions – including investigations, deportation, and intelligence – were combined with U.S. Customs investigators, the Federal Protective Service, and the Federal Air Marshall Service, to form U.S. Immigration and Customs Enforcement (ICE); and

(iii) the border functions of the INS, which included the U.S. Border Patrol as well as INS inspectors, were combined with U.S. Customs inspectors to create the U.S. Customs and Border Protection Agency (CBP).

Section 101 of Title 1 of the Homeland Security Act of 2002 outlines the "mission" of the Department of Homeland Security:

(a) Establishment – "There is established a Department of Homeland Security, as an executive department of the United States within the meaning of Title 5, United States Code.

(b) Mission

(1) In General – The primary mission of the Department is to:

(A) prevent terrorist attacks within the United States;

(B) reduce the vulnerability of the United States to terrorism, and

(C) minimize the damage, and assist in the recovery, from terrorist attacks that do occur within the United States."

The USA Patriot Act (2001)

Because of its controversial invocations, and the attention paid by the public to its implementation, a separate chapter (Chapter 19) has been set aside to discuss this controversial Act called the "USA Patriot Act" (2001).

A summary of the Act, with some facts and major provisions of it, follows:

1. The "USA PATRIOT ACT" stands for "United and Strengthening of America by

Providing Appropriate Tools Required to
Intercept and Obstruct Terrorism Act."

2. The 242-page legislation passed the House
of Representatives by a vote of 357 to 66,
and it passed the U.S. Senate by a vote of
98 to 1. It was signed into law by President
George Herbert Walker Bush (or "Bush 43")
on October 26, 2001: only 45 days after the
September 11, 2001 terrorist attacks on the
United States.

3. Some provisions of the Act were set to expire
in 2005, and were required to be acted upon
by the U.S. Congress. These provisions are
discussed in the succeeding chapter of this
book (Chapter 19).

4. The USA Patriot Act lowered the standard
for domestic surveillance in cases in which
foreign intelligence is a "significant purpose"
of an investigation. Under the previous
or old standard for domestic surveillance,
foreign intelligence had to be the "primary
purpose."

5. The Act further allows law enforcement to
share grand jury and wiretap information
concerning "foreign intelligence" without
first obtaining a court order in the appropriate
jurisdiction or venue.

6. The Patriot Act makes it easier for law
enforcement to enlist the assistance of third
parties such as landlords, and others, in

conducting court-ordered surveillance of subjects of investigation.

7. And, the Act allows the so-called "Foreign Intelligence Surveillance Court" to authorize physical searches and electronic surveillance of foreign powers' employees for up to 120 days. Previously, physical searches and electronic surveillance of this type had a limit of 45 days. The Act also allows extensions of up to 12 months.

[Source: U.S. Department of Justice; Detroit News Research; http://www.personal.umich.edu/~jeda/ PatriotActFacts.htm]

In sum, the USA Patriot Act (of 2001) is not pork or beef, nor is it chicken or turkey. It is sausage. Scary sausage.

CHAPTER NINETEEN:
The USA Patriot Act of 2001

Kindergarten Lecture

U.S. Attorney General John Ashcroft was visiting an elementary school. After a brief talk to the students about civics, the Attorney General announced, "Alright, boys and girls, you can now ask me questions."

A little boy named Charlie raised his hand and said: "Mr. Ashcroft, I have three questions. First of all, how did Mr. Bush win the election for President with less votes that Mr. Gore? Second, why are you using the USA Patriot Act to restrict or limit Americans' civil liberties? And third, why hasn't the U.S. caught Osama Bin Laden yet?"

At that very moment, the bell sounded and all the kids ran out of the school to the playground. After a few minutes, the children returned to the classroom for completion of the lecture.

A little girl raised her hand and said: "Mr. Ashcroft, I have five questions for you. First, how did Bush win the election for President with less votes that Mr. Gore? Second, why are you using the USA Patriot Act to restrict or limit Americans' civil liberties? Third, why hasn't the U.S. caught Osama Bin Laden yet?" Fourth, why did the school bell go off 20 minutes early? And fifth, where's Charlie?"

[Source: Jokes Gallery; http://www.jokesgallery. com/joke.php?joke=1646&id=1]

Background

The United States Congress passed the USA Patriot Act in response to, and very shortly after, the terrorists' attacks on the twin towers of New York City, the Pentagon in Washington, D.C., and the air over Pennsylvania on September 11, 2001. The Act gives Federal officials considerably greater authority and power to track, monitor, and intercept communications within the United States, for both law enforcement and foreign intelligence-gathering purposes.

The full title of the Act (Public Law 107-56, 115 Stat. 272 (2001)) is the "Uniting and Strengthening of American by Providing Appropriate Tools Required to Intercept and Obstruct Terrorism" Act. It was signed into law by President Bush ("number 43") on October 26, 2001, a mere 45 days after the September 11th terrorist attacks.

Under the Act the Secretary of the Treasury is given extensive new regulatory powers to combat corruption of U.S. financial institutions for foreign money laundering purposes. Border patrol and immigration officials are given further authority to close U.S. borders to foreign terrorists, and to detain and remove those terrorists within the nation's borders. Further, new crimes, new penalties, and new procedural steps are created for use against domestic and international terrorists.

The Act is not without *some* procedural safeguards for the civil liberties of United States citizens. However, in my opinion and the opinion of many others, it is still a piece of onerous legislation. Scary sausage.

The declared purpose of the USA Patriot Act is to "deter and punish American terrorists in the United States and around the world, to enhance law enforcement investigatory tools, and for other purposes." A major problem with the legislation is that it was essentially written by Republican Attorney General John Ashcroft's Justice Department. A major criticism of the Act is that "other purposes" frequently involves, thus far, the detection and prosecution of non-terrorist alleged future crimes. In other words, the Act is being used for domestic spying and information-gathering on American citizens.

Some of the controversial abuses and invocations of the USA Patriot Act include the following:

Department of Justice Audit

1. On March 9, 2007, a U.S. Department of Justice audit found that the Federal Bureau of Investigations (FBI) had "improperly and, in some cases, illegally used the [Act] to secretly obtain personal information" about United States citizens [The Guardian].

U.S. District Court Order

2. On June 15, 2007, after an internal FBI audit discovered that FBI agents had abused the Act's authority more than 1000 times, U.S. District Court Judge John D. Bates issued a court order mandating the agency

to begin turning over thousands of pages of documents related to the agency's national security "letters" program [First Amendment Center].

Summit, New Jersey and the Homeless

3. The city of Summit, New Jersey actually invoked the USA PATRIOT Act to defend itself in a lawsuit because of its actions in removing homeless people from its train station. Citing a section of the law referencing "attacks and other [actions of] violence against mass transportation systems," the city stated in its defense that its conduct was protected by the Act and that a homeless man's federal lawsuit should be dismissed. Even the Bush (#43) U.S. Justice Department criticized Summit, New Jersey's misuse of the law, stating that the city's interpretation of the Act "[represented] a fundamental misunderstanding of what the Patriot Act is."

Dismissal of the U.S. Attorneys

4. The dismissal by Republican U.S. Attorney General Alberto Gonzales' Justice Department of seven (7) United States Attorneys on Pearl Harbor Day, December 7, 2006, was another disaster connected with implementation of the USA Patriot Act. Apparently, senior members of the White House and the Department of Justice cooperated and participated in compiling the list of dismissees [See, Plan for

Replacing Certain United States Attorneys; attached to an email from Kyle Sampson to William W. Mercer, December 5, 2006].

The USA PATRIOT Act Improvement and Reauthorization Act of 2005, which was signed into law by President Bush (#43) on March 9, 2006, wiped out the previous 120-day term limit of interim U.S. Attorneys appointed to fill vacated offices. The effect of this nullification was to give the U.S. Attorney General greater appointment power for U.S. Attorneys than even the President of the United States had, since the interim U.S. Attorneys did not need U.S. Senate confirmation, but the Presidential U.S. Attorney nominees do.

It should be observed here that an interim U.S. Attorney's term expires upon the confirmation and wearing-in of a Presidentially-appointed U.S. Attorney, if one is put forward by the President. Critics and opponents have argued that the dismissals were either politically-motivated by the desire and intent to install U.S. Attorneys more loyal to the Republican Party, or as punishment for actions or inactions of the seven U.S. Attorneys believed to be damaging to the Party. Again, it should be mentioned that at least six of the eight dismissed U.S. Attorneys had positive internal Department of Justice performance reviews [David Johnston, "Reviews of 6 fired attorneys positive," Washington Post, 02/25/2007].

Finally, after extensive Congressional hearings, the "Preserving United States Attorney Independent Act of 2007" was filed by Congress in January 2007, and it signed into law by President Bush in June 14, 2007. The new law rescinded the "no-term-limit" interim U.S.

Attorney provision of the USA PATRIOT Act, and it specifies that all Attorney General-appointed interim U.S. Attorneys then in office and forward shall have a term that ends 120 days from the signing of the bill into law.

Investigation of Potential Drug Dealers

5. The *New York Times* newspaper, in September 2003, reported on one of several cases of the USA PATRIOT Act being used to investigate and prosecute alleged domestic potential drug dealers "without probable cause." The article also mentions a study by Congress that referenced hundreds of cases where the Act was used to investigate and prosecute "non-terrorist alleged future crimes." The *New York Times* reported that these non-terrorist investigations are relevant because President Bush and several members of the U.S. Congress had declared that the purpose of the USA PATRIOT Act was that of investigating and preempting potential terrorist acts [New York Times, September 28, 2003].

Viva **Las Vegas**

6. In a November 2005 issue of *Business Week* magazine, it was reported that the Federal Bureau of Investigation (FBI) had issued tens of thousands of "National Security Letters" and had obtained over one million financial records from the customers of targeted Las Vegas businesses. The targeted business included casinos, storage warehouses, and

car rental agencies. The FBI alleges that its authority to seek this private information of American citizens was grounded in Section 505 of the USA PATRIOT Act. Other private information of American citizens accessed by the FBI include credit records, employment records, and health records. And worse, this information is databased and maintained indefinitely by the FBI and other government agencies within the Department of Homeland Security.

Public Libraries

7. One of America's most sacred institutions, the public library, has also been victimized by the USA PATRIOT Act. Our public libraries are under demand from the FBI to release their records on library patrons. Several libraries have filed lawsuits, since the "national security letters" served on them by the FBI have been widely sweeping in scope, demanding personal information not just on the individual patron under investigation, but also on everyone who had used specific terminals at the libraries during stated time periods. Since many of these affected library patrons and terminal users are minor children, same libraries have felt a responsibility or obligation to notify the parents of this minors regarding the FBI's inquiries and demands for information. The public libraries' lawsuits are still working their way through the courts.

Other Examples of Abuse

8. There are numerous other examples of controversial abuses and invocations of the USA PATRIOT Act, including: wrongful investigations into alleged copyright infringement (the Act amended the Computer Fraud and Abuse Act to include search and seizure of records from Internet Service Providers); wrongful investigations and accusations of citizen violations of Section 175 of the U.S. Biological Weapons Anti-Terrorism Act (a law which was expanded by the USA PATRIOT Act); and unlawful domestic surveillance on American citizens for lengthy periods of time without proper authority [Dan Eggen, "FBI Papers Indicate Intelligence Violations Secret Surveillance Lacked Oversight," *Washington Post*, October 23, 2005], among other incidents.

U.S. Immigration and the USA Patriot Act

It is undisputed that United States immigration policy played a major role in allowing foreign terrorists to enter the U.S. and conduct terrorist activities before and during "9/11/2001." Despite that fact, the USA PATRIOT Act does little to improve immigration policy in this regard. The few immigration provisions included in the Act reveal two consistent and increasingly problematic views on American immigration policy which appear to be shared by the U.S. Congress and the U.S. Department of Justice, to wit:

<u>View #1</u> that the United States Citizenship and Immigration Service's (USCIS's) main function is the admission of aliens into the United States, instead of the enforcement of the immigration laws regulating such alien admissions; and

<u>View #2</u> that American immigration policy is a political wasteland subject to government benign neglect and better left untouched.

View #1 is manifested by the USA PATRIOT Act's failure to recognize that enforcement of existing American immigration laws is just as important in the so-called "war on terrorism" as better foreign intelligence and more diligent prosecution of those with ties to terrorists, and the failure of the Act to hold the USCIS (as well as the EOIR) accountable for such enforcement [<u>Center for Immigration Studies</u>, "The USA PATRIOT Act" of 2001, December 2001].

View #2 is revealed throughout the immigration-related parts of the Act. Instead of requiring imminent action by the USCIS or EOIR and the State Department, several provisions merely mandate "studies" of potential future actions. Therefore, instead of requiring that USCIS and EOIR immediately institute appropriate programs enacted by the U.S. Congress in 1996, the Act requires simple "progress reports" [<u>CIS</u>, **Ibid**].

The more chilling effort of the USA PATRIOT Act of 2001 has been on the civil liberties of American citizens.

CHAPTER TWENTY:
American Immigration and
The USA Patriot Act of 2001

The [US] Senate has passed a resolution to make English the official language of the United States. Today President Bush said this is the "goodest news" he's heard in a long time [by Jay Leno, late night comedian]; and "President Bush [also] said making English our national language is not 'discriminatious'" [by Conan O'Brien, late-night comedian].

"Immigration is the big issue right now. Earlier today, the [U.S. Congress] voted to build a 370-mile fence along the Mexico border...Experts say a 370-mile fence is the perfect way to protect a border [with Mexico] that is 1,900 miles long" [Conan O'Brien, late-night TV show host].

In terms of its real effect on American immigration policy and practice, the USA PATRIOT ACT of 2001 has had a negligible or *de minimis* impact. The Act does contain a number of provisions that are allegedly designed to thwart terrorist attacks and to "prevent" terrorists from entering the United States from Canada and Mexico, but it is lacking in meaningful immigration substance.

BORDER PATROL AND PROTECTION

Under the U.S. Border patrol and protection provisions of the Act:

(i) authorization is given for "appropriations necessary" to triple the number of Border Patrol, Customs Service, and Immigration and Naturalization (INS) personnel stationed along the Northern Border with Canada (Section 401 of the Act);

(ii) Section 402 of the Act authorizes appropriations of an additional $50 million for both INS [USCIS] and the Customers Service to upgrade border surveillance equipment;

(iii) Section 404 removed for fiscal year 2001 the $30,000 cap on border patrol overtime pay for INS employees;

(iv) $2 million was authorized for a "report" to be prepared by the Attorney General of the United States on the feasibility of enhancing the FBI's Integrated Automated Fingerprint Identification System (IAFIS) and similar systems to improve the reliability of visa applicant screening (Section 405 of the Act).

(v) Section 403 authorized the appropriations necessary to provide the State Department and INS with criminal record identification information relating to visa applicants and other applicants for admission to the United States;

(vi) Section 1007 of the Act instructs the Attorney General to "report" on the feasibility of the use of a biometric identifier scanning system with access to IAFIS (Integrated Automated Fingerprint Identification System) for overseas consular posts and points of entry into the United States;

(vii) the Secretary of State is directed to determine whether consular shopping is a problem, to take any necessary corrective action, and to "report" the action taken (Section 418 of the Act);

(viii) the "sense of the Congress" is expressed that the Administration of President Bush ("#43") should implement the integrated entry and exit data system called for by the Illegal Immigration Reform and Immigration Responsibility Act of 1996 (8 U.S.C. 1365a), pursuant to Section 414 of the Act;

(ix) the White House Office of Homeland Security is added to the Integrated Entry and Exit Data System Task Force (8 U.S.C. 1365a, note), pursuant to Section 415 of the Act;

(x) implementation and expansion of the foreign student visa monitoring programs is "called for" (8 U.S.C. 1372), pursuant to Section 416 of the Act;

(xi) it is requested of the Administration that countries eligible to participate in the visa waiver program be limited to those with "machine-readable passports" as of October 1, 2003 (8

U.S.C. 1187(c)), pursuant to Section 417 of the Act;

(xii) the Attorney General is instructed to "report" on the feasibility of using biometric scanners to help prevent terrorists and other foreign criminals from entering the United States, pursuant to Section 1008 of the Act;

[As the House Judiciary Committee explained, "A biometric fingerprint scanning system is a sophisticated computer scanning technology that analyzes a person's fingerprint and compares the measurement with a verified sample digitally stored in the system. The accuracy of these systems is claimed to be above 99.9%. The biometric identifier system contemplated by this section would have access to the database of the Federal Bureau of Investigation Integrated Automated Fingerprint Identification System," H.R. Rep. No. 107-236, at 78 (2001); CRS Report for Congress, Congressional Research Service, the Library of Congress, April 15, 2002, Order Code RL 31377].

(xiii) appropriations of $250,000 were authorized for the Federal Bureau of Investigation (FBI) to determine the feasibility of providing commercial airlines with computer access to the names, etc., of suspected terrorists, under Section 1009 of the Act; and

(xiv) authorization was given for reciprocal sharing of the State Department's visa lookout data and related information with other countries in order to prevent terrorism, during trafficking, slave marketing, and gun running, pursuant to Section 413 of the Act [Charles Doyle, Senior Specialist, American Law Division, CRS, The Library of Congress, "The USA PATRIOT Act: A Legal Analysis," April 15, 2002, Order Code RL 31377].

DETENTION AND REMOVAL OF ALIENS

Foreign nationals, or aliens, are "deportable" or removable from the United States, among other reasons, if they were inadmissible at the time they entered the country or if they have subsequently engaged in terrorist activity [8 U.S.C. 1227(a)(1)(A), (a)(4)(B), 1182(a)(3) (B)(iv)].

Aliens, or foreign nationals, may be inadmissible for any number of terrorism-related reasons or grounds [8 U.S.C. 1182(a)(3)(B)]. Section 411 of the USA Patriot Act adds to the terrorism-related grounds or reasons upon which an alien may be denied admission into the United States, and consequently upon which she or he may be removed or deported.

Prior to the Immigration Act of 1990 (P.L. 101-649) there was really no particularized terrorism-related ground for exclusion from the United States. Congress actually added the terrorism ground in the 1990 Act as part of a broader effort to "streamline and modernize the security and foreign policy [reasons or] grounds for inadmissibility and removal" [Michael John Garcia and Ruth Ellen Wasem, CRS, the Library of Congress, "Immigration: Terrorist Grounds for Exclusion and Removal of Aliens," January 22, 2008, Order Code RL

3256]. Before 1990, certain terrorists were excludable under security reasons, but the 1990 Act opened the door for more expansive elaboration of which associations and promotional activities could be deemed to be terrorist activities.

In 1993 the World Trade Center bombing spurred Congress to strengthen the anti-terrorism provisions in the Immigration and Nationality Act (INA). Congress further voted in legislations that many felt would step-up terrorist enforcement activities, such as the controversial Illegal Immigration Reform and Immigrant Responsibility Act (IIRIRA) of 1996, the so-called "Ira-Ira" law (P.L. 104-208), and the Antiterrorism and Effective Death Penalty Act (P.L. 104-132). Both of these laws have faced substantial legal challenges in Federal courts.

In 1994, as part of the Violent Crime Control Act of 1994 (P. L. 103-322), Congress amended the Immigration and Naturalization (INA) to establish temporary authority for an "S" nonimmigrant visa category and aliens who are witnesses and informants on criminal and terrorist activities. In September 2001, Congress passed "S.1424" (P.L. 107-45), which provides permanent authority for admission under the S visa [CRS Report, RS 21043, "Immigration: S Visas for Criminal and Terrorist Informants," by Karma Ester]. Shortly thereafter, in October 2001, the USA PATRIOT Act (P.L. 107-56) was enacted.

The Enhanced Border Security and Visa Entry Reform Act of 2002 (P.L. 107-173), or "EBSVERA," was subsequently enacted with the goal of improving the visa issuance process out of the country as well as immigration inspections at America's borders [CRS Report, RS21438, "Immigration Legislation Enacted in the 107th Congress," by Andovia Bruno]. In 2004, the Intelligence Reform and Terrorism Prevention Act (P.L. 108-458), IRTPA, was passed, focusing primarily on targeting terrorist travel through an intelligence and security strategy based allegedly on reliable identification systems and effective, integrated information-sharing. IRTPA's immigration provisions are aimed at more strict monitoring of persons lawfully entering and leaving the United States as well as tightening up the grounds for removal. The law also authorized an increase in the budget for "immigration-related homeland security."

On May 11, 2005, the REAL ID Act of 2005 was signed into law by President Bush (#43). The new Federal law imposes several security, authentication and issuance procedures and standards for state driver's licenses and state ID cards. The primary stated purpose for the Act is to create ID for "official purposes," as defined by the Secretary of Homeland Security. The REAL ID Act of 2005 is a rider to an act of Congress entitled the "Emergency Supplemental Appropriations Act for Defense, the Global War on Terror, Tsunami Relief, 2005."

The REAL ID Act also instituted the following changes.

(i) changed visa limits for temporary workers, nurses, and Australian citizens;

(ii) waived laws that hindered construction of physical barriers at the borders;

(iii) funded some "reports" and "pilot projects" related to border security;

(iv) introduced rules covering "delivery bonds," rather similar to bail bonds, with the difference that "delivery bonds" are for aliens who have been released pending immigration hearings, etc.;

(v) established new national standards for state-issued driver licenses and non-driver identification cards; and

(vi) updated and tightened the laws on application for asylum and deportation of aliens suspected of terrorist activity.

Proponents of the REAL ID Act voice similar arguments to those made in favor of the USA Patriot Act, that both laws are needed to combat both terrorists and illegal immigrants. Opponents of these laws agree that the REAL ID Act imposes more onerous requirements for identity documents on the states, and gives the Department of Homeland Security far more power than necessary to do what needs to be done to protect our nation's national security.

In 2008, the Consolidated Appropriations Act (P.L. 110-161) was enacted to modify the application of certain terrorism-related provisions of the Immigration and Nationality Act (INA). Among other things, this Act exempted ten (10) organizations from falling under the definition of "terrorist organization" and it expanded the authority of immigration authorities to waive authority over many terrorism-related INA provisions.

CHAPTER TWENTY-ONE:
Current Immigration Issues in the United States

The Agenda – "Immigration" – The White House

IMMIGRATION

"The time to fix our broken immigration system is now...We need stronger enforcement on the border and at the workplace...But for reform to work, we also must respond to what pulls people to America...Where we can reunited families, we should. Where we can bring in more foreign-born workers with the skills our economy needs, we should." – Barack Obama, Statement on U.S. Senate Floor May 23, 2007.

For too long, politicians in Washington have exploited the immigration issue to divide the nation rather than find real solutions. Our broken immigration system can only be fixed by putting politics aside and offering a complete solution that secures our border, enforces our laws, and reaffirms our heritage as a nation of immigrants.

Create Secure Borders: Protect the integrity of our borders. Support additional personnel, infrastructure and technology on the border and at our ports of entry.

Improve Our Immigration System: Fix the dysfunctional immigration bureaucracy and increase the number of legal immigrants to keep families together and meet the demand for jobs that employers cannot fill.

Remove Incentives to Enter Illegally: Remove incentives to enter the country illegally by cracking down on employers who hire undocumented immigrants.

Bring People Out of the Shadows: Support a system that allows undocumented immigrants who are in good standing to pay a fine, learn English and go to the back of the line for the opportunity to become citizens.

Work with Mexico: Promote economic development in Mexico to decrease illegal immigration.

(Source: The White House Website, January 22, 2009; http://www.whitehouse.gov/agenda/immigration]

Former United States Senator, and now 44th President of the United States, Barack Obama is a very bright and thoughtful person. A thinker who also follows with appropriate action. If the U.S. congress is ready to focus on serious solutions to our nation's immigration issues, I believe President Obama is willing and able to work cooperatively with it.

It appears to many that by now having and enforcing reasonable immigration policies and practices, the United States has, probably through benign neglect, created a system that practically begs for aliens to break the laws of our country. This nation, again, creates a paradox in immigration policy and practice.

Current Immigration History

I believe and propose that we are now in the fifth (5th) period of American immigration history: the "post-9/11/2001" period. The fifth period began, of course, during the Administration of President Bush (#43) and it is continuing under the new Administration of President Barack Obama. As we have shown in Chapters 17, 18, 19 and 20, *supra*, the nature of new legislation ostensibly affecting immigration since September 11, 2001, assuming implementation, invariably impacts and changes American immigration policies and practices.

Consequently, I propose that American immigration history can practically be seen in five (5) periods:

(1) the Colonial period (from about the 1500s to the mid-1800s) brought the Europeans;

(2) the mid-nineteenth century (mid-1800s) to about the 1900s, or turn of the twentieth century, saw mainly an influx from Northern Europe;

(3) the turn of the twentieth century, or about the 1900s to about 1965, brought a substantial number of Southern and Eastern Europeans;

(4) the post-1965 to September 11, 2001 period featured immigrants primarily from Latin America and Asia; and

(5) the post-September 11, 2001 period is currently under development.

Current immigrants to the United States settle primarily in twelve (12) states:

STATE	2007 Immigrant Population
1. California	9,980,000
2. New York	4,105,000
3. Florida	3,453,000
4. Texas	3,438,000
5. New Jersey	1,869,000
6. Illinois	1,702,000
7. Georgia	953,000
8. Massachusetts	897,000
9. Arizona	891,000
10. Virginia	856,000
11. Maryland	731,000
12. Washington	722,000

[Sources: Center for Immigration Studies (CIS), 2008; U.S. Census Population Surveys, 2007]

These states are all high foreign-born population sites, together representing more than half of the United States population in whole. Of those individuals who immigrated to America in very recent times, better than 58% were from Latin America.

Currently the top ten counties from which immigrants come into the Untied States are:

COUNTRY	Number of Immigrants Who Entered the U.S.
1. Mexico	11,671,000
2. China	2,007,000

133

COUNTRY	Number of Immigrants Who Entered the U.S.
3. India	1,704,000
4. Philippines	1,665,000
5. Vietnam	999,000
6. El Salvador	998,000
7. Cuba	980,000
8. Former USSR	973,000
9. Korea	906,000
10. Dominican Republic	856,000

[Sources: Center for Immigration Studies (CIS), March 2007]

Proponents of immigration argue, among other things, that immigration is the driving force behind America's growth. Opponents naturally argue that America needs to get its growth under control now, and stop "illegal" or "undocumented" alien intrusion immediately.

"Undocumented" or So-called "Illegal" Immigration ("Unauthorized Immigration")

The phrase "unauthorized immigration" is also used to identify or describe this "act of foreign nationals violating United States immigration policies and national laws by immigrating to the United States without proper consent from the United States government" [Source: USCIS].

Depending upon the credible source of data, the 'unauthorized,' "illegal," or "undocumented" immigrant population of the Untied States is estimated to be between 12 and 15 million people. It is estimated that 57 percent of "unauthorized" migrants are from Mexico; 24 percent are from other Latin American countries, principally from Central America; 9 percent are from Asia; 6 percent are from Europe and Canada; and 4 percent are from the remainder of the world [Source: "Illegal Immigrants in the U.S.: How many are there?," by Brad Knickerbocker, *The Christian Science Monitor*, May 16, 2006: Estimates of the Size and Characteristics of the Undocumented Population – Full Report" (PDF), Pew Hispanic Center, March 21, 2005].

A listing of the distribution of "Unauthorized Immigrants," by state in the United States, follows as of 2006:

State of Residence of "Unauthorized Immigrant Population" (2006)	Estimated Population (2006)	Percent of Total U.S. "Unauthorized Immigrant Population" (2006)
(1) California	2,830,000	25%
(2) Texas	1,640,000	14%
(3) Florida	980,000	8%
(4) Illinois	550,000	5%
(5) New York	540,000	5%
(6) Arizona	500,000	4%
(7) Georgia	490,000	4%
(8) New Jersey	430,000	4%
(9) North Carolina	370,000	3%
(10) Washington	280,000	2%
(11) Other States	2,950,000	26%
Total (All States)	11,550,000	100%

[Sources: <u>Fact Sheet</u>, April 26, 2006, Pew Hispanic Center; "Estimating the Undocumented Population," GAO (Government Accountability Office), September 2006; <u>Estimates of the Unauthorized Immigrant Population Residing in the United States</u>: January 2006, Michael Hoefer, Nancy Rytina and Christopher Campbell, Office of Immigration Statistics (August 2007)]

Current Public Opinion and Current Controversy Regarding "Unauthorized Immigration"

As evidenced by discussions in the media, and as I recently witnessed in spirited email discussions in an online network of a state bar association, the differing beliefs among Americans concerning "unauthorized immigration" is stark and widespread.

Supporters of "unauthorized immigration" argue, among other things, that unauthorized immigrants:

– keep the American economy flowing by taking low-waged jobs that few Americans take;

– provide consumers with better goods and services;

– still pay sales taxes;

– pay other taxes such as real estate taxes if they own property; and

– fulfill the ideology of the "American Dream."

Opponents of "unauthorized immigration" argue among other things, that unauthorized immigrants:

– are law-breakers by definition;

– take jobs needed by Americans;

– create a burden on taxpayers;

– cause harm and even death to themselves by crossing the border illegally; and

– cause crime to escalate in local communities, as well as increase health risks to others (e.g., lack of vaccinations, etc.).

The higher level of public opinion about "unauthorized immigrants" usually comes down to the issue of jobs, or the level of employment. Pro-immigrant sentiment is usually higher in areas where unemployment is lower, and anti-immigrant sentiment is usually higher in areas where unemployment is higher ["Immigration and Public Opinion," Maryanne Belanger and Thomas J. Espenshade (1998); CBS News/New York Times Poll, May 18-23,2007].

There is much to criticize about United States immigration policy and practice. Despite criticism on all sides, however, on balance America is generally considered still to be probably among the more receptive major nations for immigration.

CHAPTER TWENTY-TWO: Fifteen (15) Tips for Winning Immigration Cases

1. Preparation. Preparation. Preparation.

There is absolutely no substitute for proper preparation of the immigration case. This involves work and effort.

2. Seek qualified legal immigration assistance and help with even what appears to be the simplest immigration request or filing. Immigration is a surprisingly complex and complicated field of law, with many pit falls for the unwary or uninformed.

3. Immigration filings for relief and/or accommodation are "form" and "fee" driven. The applicant for immigration relief must file accurately the proper form and pay the proper fee for consideration. And, there are no guarantees of success. The USCIS (United States Citizenship and Immigration Services), particularly, is "form" and "fee" driven. In fact, the filing fees are the major revenue source for the USCIS.

4. Qualified immigration attorney or lawyer assistance is especially recommended for representation in hearings before U.S. Immigration Judges (IJs) or any other matter within the jurisdiction of the EOIR (Executive Office for Immigration Review). Good immigration lawyering can make a major difference here.

5. Check the professional background and ask questions when choosing which immigration attorney to hire. Just because an attorney has membership in a particular organization does not necessarily mean that attorney is the right choice for you and your immigration issue.

Remember that the "cheapest" is not usually the best. If an immigration attorney is much less expensive than anyone else, there is probably a reason. Usually, if you want quality, you have to pay a little more for it. Obtaining a visa or permanent residence in the United States is often a once in a lifetime opportunity. Don't ruin your chances just because you want to save a few dollars.

6. Read carefully and follow the instructions on the immigration forms in detail and with specificity. Remember that immigration instructions and forms are the law. Follow both carefully.

Read the instructions on the forms carefully for specific information regarding the requirements for each petition or application. Then, after the forms have been completed, **double-check** everything to make sure that you didn't leave anything out. If you are unsure about how to answer a specific question, check with a competent immigration attorney, or knowledgeable representative, or appropriate government employee for help. **Never** answer a question on a form unless you **know** all of the consequences of your answer.

7. Precision, Correctness, and Timeliness in immigration filing and processing by applicants is crucial. Remember to send with your completed forms

the correct filing fees for each application or petition, and make sure you have included all of the required additional documents.

If an incorrect filing fee is sent, the Immigration Service will return the documents to you and your case will not be accepted for processing. Since it often takes the Immigration Service 30 days or more to return the forms, you may now be out of status, i.e., in an unlawful or unauthorized or illegal status. Therefore, even if you return the forms with the proper fees, your case may be denied because it was filed late. Also, if you do not enclose all of the documents requested, an additional request will be made to you, which will significantly delay the processing of your case. And may even end your chances for approval or acceptance.

8. Delivering or mailing your petition, application and other forms to the proper or correct immigration address is, again, critical to the success of your case.

If the Immigration Service does not receive the application at the correct office, it will not accept your case and the forms will be returned to you at some point. Once again, you may now be out of status and your case can be denied because it was filed late. Since government addresses are constantly changing, it is a good idea to check with the appropriate government agency prior to submitting your application in order to make sure you are sending your documents to the proper address.

9. As in the case of most things in life, timing is very important. Be sure you have filed and acted in a timely manner. Procrastination can be fatal to your immigration case.

In the field of Immigration, everything that is filed has a deadline. If you miss the deadline, it is very likely that your application or petition will be denied and, depending on the type of application or petition, there may be no opportunity to appeal. In addition, if you fall out of status, you may become subject to the three and ten year bars, and/or any visas you have will be considered void.

10. Immigration "priority dates" are an important (pardon the pun) priority. Be sure your priority date is current. You can obtain current information on the most current priority dates from several sources, including the USCIS, EOIR, and other immigration websites – both governmental sites and non-governmental sites.

Prior to filing your case, you should check the above-references sources to make sure that the date applicable has been reached in your preference category.

If you file your petition or application before the date is current, it will be rejected by the Immigration Service or State Department, and not only will you have wasted your time and money, but some of the documents may have become outdated and will have to be obtained again.

11. Receipts for filings are necessary. Get a receipt for anything and everything you mail or deliver to Homeland Security, USCIS, EOIR, INS, the Immigration Court, the U.S. Department of Labor, the State Department, U.S. Consuls, and anyone else involved in your case.

These agencies frequently have an uncanny way of losing or misplacing your documents. If you don't get a receipt, and if there is no canceled check or money order, it will be impossible to prove that your documents were received. These government agencies will not take your word for it. They want to see a receipt. And you will regret it if you do not have one.

12. Send original documents only if they are absolutely required or mandated by the rules or law. And make copies to keep of everything you file.

As we have stated previously in 11, above, government agencies have a notorious reputation for losing your valuable paperwork and other things. Further, when a case is finished they do *not* return the original documents to you. Some of these documents are one of a kind and cannot be replaced, or are extremely hard to replace. In most cases, you will be permitted to certify on your application or petition that the document is a true copy of the original. If the original document is required, make sure you send both the original as well as a copy. Make sure you supply a stamped self-addressed return envelope and ask the agency to return the originals to you when they are completed with it. While this will not guarantee that you will get it back, it will significantly improve your chances.

13. What should you do if your case is returned to you for more information? First, seek competent legal assistance, since Immigration or some other agency is obviously not satisfied with what you originally provided. Secondly, whether with counsel or not, make sure you respond to each point, even if you have already provided the information. If Immigration or another agency took the time to write you back for specific information, it

is because they obviously were not satisfied with what you originally provided, or because they didn't see it. So answer each point in detail. If you don't supply the information requested, there is a very good chance your case will be denied.

14. Do not file your case and then simply hope that the stars will align in your favor. Engage in frequent follow-up on your case.

If you just sit and wait for a response, you could wait forever, because, as stated above, your documents could be lost or misplaced. If your receipt gives normal processing times, then do not check before the time given. However, if you have not received any type of response within the normal time frame, check on your case immediately. Make sure you get a response to your request, and keep a record of all contacts you make with the government agencies.

15. Follow this summary bottom-line check list of things "to do:"

(a) Always be sure you have all the facts at your disposal [1 and 6, *supra*].

(b) Always provide all information as requested [1, 6 and 7, *supra*].

(c) Never, never lie on any of the forms you file [1 and 14, *supra*].

(d) Always follow through with all required steps [1 and 14, *supra*].

(e) Always be timely in your filings and actions [7 and 9, *supra*].

(f) Be persistent in your efforts [1 and 14, *supra*].

(g) Never alienate or otherwise be disrespectful to immigration authorities and others involved in your immigration case. They will have the last laugh...at your expense [1 and 14, *supra*].

(h) Always keep copies of everything you send to immigration officials and others involved in your immigration case [11 and 12, *supra*].

(i) Beware of exorbitant immigration scams, schemes, and promises. If it sounds too good to be true, then it is probably not true.

Good-Luck!

ABOUT THE AUTHOR

Charles Ware is a former United States Immigration Judge. He is currently a principal in the national general practice law firm of Charles Jerome Ware, Attorneys & Counsellors. He has published and spoken publicly numerous times on various legal topics. His previous legal book published by iUniverse in 2008, "Understanding the Law: A Primer," has been well-received by readers. He is a former college administrator and university law professor. Charles Ware has been featured on his own number one legal advice radio program, as well as numerous other television and radio shows. He lives in Columbia, Maryland with his wife Fran, and his daughter Lucinda-Marie.

INDEX

Author's Note

- "An Immigration Paradox develops when American immigration policy is subjected to Government benign neglect." – Charles Jerome Ware, Former U.S. Immigration Judge;

- "In America, no human being is "illegal;"

- Immigration: the movement of persons into a foreign country for the purpose of permanently residing in that country;

- Conservative estimates place our nation's documented and undocumented (so-called "unauthorized") immigrant population at over forty millions persons;

- "Nothing Is Too Late" (Book), by Mark E. Kalmansohn, 2004, Brassey's Inc.'

- "Understanding The Law: A Primer" (Book), by Attorney Charles Jerome Ware, 2008; iUniverse Press, www.amazon.com;

- Christian Brown Associates, www.ourchanceforlove.com

- WWW.CHARLESJEROMEWARE.COM

Chapter 1 – Immigration Humor.

- U.S. President William Jefferson Clinton;
- United States Congress;
- "Top Ten Foreign Countries-Foreign Born Population Among U.S. Immigrants" [A Chart];

Chapter 2 – Native Americans.

- Beringia
- "Special" Status of Native Americans (American Indians);
- 1924 Citizenship of American Indians by the Congress of the United States;
- Christopher Columbus

Chapter 3 – Black American Indians.

- Black American Indians
- Hispaniola; Dominican Republic; Puerto Rico; "New World;"
- African slaves; Native Americans;
- South Carolina; Virginia; New York;
- Iroquois Indians; Cherokee Indians; Huron Indians; Delaware Indians;
- The British Governor of New York;
- "Upper South;"
- European Colony of Jamestown, Virginia;

Chapter 4 – Beringia and the Bering Strait.

- Beringia; Bering Strait; "Bering land bridge;"

- Alaska; Eastern Siberia; Pleistocene Ice Ages; Eurasia; Chukchi Sea; Bering Sea; Russia; Siberia; Artic Circle;

- Danish-born Russian Mariner Vitus Bering;

Chapter 5 – Mariel: The Cuban Boatlift Crisis.

- President Jimmy Carter

- The Cuban Boatlift Crisis

- The Mariel BoatLift

- Cuba; Cubans; Cuban President Fidel Castro;

- The Cuban Boatlift Project;

- Southern Florida; Havana Cuba

- Peruvian Embassy in Cuba; Embassy of Venezuela, Marimar, Cuba;

- "Open-Arms" immigration policy;

- "Lumpens;"

- 1882 "Head Tax" of the U.S. Congress;

- "Cuban Immigrant Arrivals on the Beaches of South Florida (Miami) during the Mariel (Cuban) Boatlift, by Month (1980)" [A Chart];

Chapter 6 – The Cuban Immigration Paradox.

- The Cuban Immigration Paradox;

- U.S. President Jimmy Carter;

- Mariel Boatlift; "Freedom Flotilla;"

- "Marielitos;" "undesirables;" excludable aliens;

- Immigration and Naturalization Service (INS);

- Immigration Reform and Control Act of 1986;

- "political prisoners;" INS policies and procedures;

- "illegal aliens;" "persons" under the United States Constitution;

- Oakdale, Louisiana; Atlanta, Georgia federal penitentiary; gangster Al Capone;

- United States Immigration Judge pursuant to Sections 101 and 103 of the Immigration and Naturalization Act, 28 CFR 0.105, and 8 CFR 2.1;

- "Scarface;" Cuban Marielito;

- Clark versus Martinez, U.S. Supreme Court case;

- Cuban refugees Sergio Suarez Martinez and Daniel Benitez;

149

Chapter 7 – The Haitian Immigration Paradox.

- The Haitian Immigration Paradox;

- Republican Nixon Administration (early 1970s);

- Haitian "boat people;"

- President Jimmy Carter;

- Republican President Ronald Reagan;

- use of U.S. Coast Guard to "intercept" Haitians;

- "interdiction" and "escorting" by U.S. Coast Guard of Haitian vessels;

- The Reagan Administration;

- repatriation of Haitian refugees;

- Haitian President Aristide; Jean-Bertrand Aristide (born July 15, 1953); Roman Catholic Priest; President of Haiti, 1991, 1994-1996, 2001-2004;

- Haitian leader Francois Duvalier;

- South Africa;

- Attorney General Griffin Bell, retired U.S. Court of Appeals Judge;

- §§ 207-208 of the Immigration and Nationality Act (INA), as amended by the Refugee Act of 1980;

- Immigration Reform and Control Act (IRCA) 1986;

- Legal Permanent Residents (LPRs);
- Homeland Security Act of 2002 (P.L. 107-296);
- "Post-9/11" environment;
- Democrat Barack Obama, 44th President of the United States;
- Department of Homeland Security (DHS);
- Immigration and Naturalization Service (INS);
- Coast Guard (interdiction): Customs and Border Protection (apprehensions and inspections); Immigration and Customs Enforcement (ICE) detention; Citizenship and Immigration Services (credible fear determination);
- Department of Justice (DOJ) Executive Office for Immigration Review (EOIR), asylum and removal hearings
- U.S. Coast Guard Interdiction of Haitians, 1982-2004 [Graphs];

Chapter 8 – Cubans versus Haitians: Disparate Immigration Treatment?

- The Cuban Adjustment Act (CAA) of 1966 (P.L. 89-732);
- "wet foot/dry foot" practice toward Cuban migrants;
- Department of Homeland Security (DHS);

- Public Law Number 89-732, Cuban Adjustment Act (CAA), November 2, 1966;
- President Lyndon Johnson;
- President Jimmy Carter;
- The Clinton Administration in the 1990s'
- "Mariel" Boatlift Crisis;

Chapter 9 – Getting Asylum.

- Asylum; Asylum cases;
- "affirmative asylum process;" "defensive asylum process;"
- United States Citizenship and Immigration Services (USCIS);
- Executive Office for Immigration Review (EOIR);
- Form I-589, Application for Asylum and for Withholding of Removal to USCIS;
- Immigration Judge (IJ) at the Executive Office for Immigration Review (EOIR);
- Immigration and Customs Enforcement (ICE);
- Board of Immigration Appeals (BIA);
- U.S. Court of Appeals;
- Import Distinctions Between "Affirmative" and "Defensive" Asylum Processes [Chart]
- "persecution" or "legitimate fear of persecution;

Chapter 10 – The Curious Case of "Joc Joc".

- Asylum cases;

- "persecution" or "legitimate fear of persecution;"

- asylum applicant Joselyn Bolante; undersecretary of the Philippine Department of Agriculture;

- Reelection Committee for Philippine President Arroyo;

- Philippine Senate; U.S. Embassy in Manila;

- Board of Immigration Appeals (BIA);

- U.S. Court of Appeals; Joselyn Bolante vs. Attorney General Mukasey, No. 07-2550, August 27, 2008, CA7;

Chapter 11 – A Primer on "Temporary Protected Status" (TPS)

- "Temporary Protected Status" (TPS);

- Section 244 of the Immigration and Nationality Act (INA);

- Immigration Act of 1990 ("IMMACT"), P.L. 101-649;

- Homeland Security Act of 2002, Public Law 107-296;

- U.S. Citizenship and Immigration Services (USCIS)

- U.S. Department of Homeland Security ("DHS");

- Secretary of Homeland Security;

- Form I-821, Application for Temporary Protected Status;

- Form I-765, Application of Employment Authorization;

- 8 CFR § 244;

- INA Section 244©(2) and 8 CFR §§ 244.1-244.4;

- Sierra Leone; Burundi; El Salvador; Honduras; Nicaragua; Somalia; Sudan; and Liberia;

- "Deferred Enforced Departure" (DED);

Chapter 12 – The "Green Card" is Not Green.

- "Green Card;" Permanent Resident Card;

- Immigration and Naturalization Service (INS);

- U.S. Department of Justice;

- Bureau of Citizenship and Immigration Services (BCIS);

- U.S. Department of Homeland Security (DHS);

- 2003 Homeland Security Reorganization;

- U.S. Citizenship and Immigration Services (USCIS);

- Employment Authorization Document (EAD);

- "Advance Parole"

- "H1-B visa, specialty occupation;

- "White Card," 1940; Permanent Resident Card;

- Biometric data;

- Ways to obtain Permanent Resident Status [List];

- Permanent Resident Eligibility and Estimated Quotas [List];

- The Heroes Earnings Assistance and Relief Acts of 1008 (The HEART Act);

- Internal Revenue Service (IRS);

Chapter 13 – The United States Immigration Judge.

- United States Immigration Judge;

- Immigration and Naturalization (INS) Commissioner David Crosland;

- Cuban (or Mariel) Boatlift Crisis;

- Atlanta Federal Penitentiary;

- Bureau of Prisons;

- Office of the Chief Immigration Judge (OCIJ);

- Executive Office for Immigration Review (EOIR); U.S. Department of Justice; Attorney General of the United States;

- Board of Immigration Appeals (BIA);

- Removal or "Deportation;"

- United Nations Convention Against Torture;

- Criminal Alien Program;

- Department of Homeland Security (DHS);

- Asylum and the Immigration Court;

- United Nations Conventions;

- U.S. Immigration Court;

- United States Citizenship and Immigration Services (USCIS);

- Asylum Seekers by Nationality;

- China; Columbia; Haiti; Albania; India; El Salvador; Mexico; Afghanistan; Burma;

- Importance of Legal Representation;

- Requests for Asylum in the United States [Chart], 2000-2005;

Chapter 14 – The United States Citizen and Immigration Service (USCIS)

- United States Citizen and Immigration Service (USCIS);

- "9/11" (2001) terrorist attacks on the United States;

- The Homeland Security Act of 2002;

- The U.S. Department of Homeland Security (DHS);

- U.S. Immigration and Naturalization Service (INS);

- Mission of the USCIS;
- Functions of the USCIS;
- U.S. Immigration and Customs Enforcement (ICE);
- Executive Office for Immigration Review (EOIR);
- United States Immigration Judges (IJs);
- Board of Immigration Appeals (BIA);

Chapter 15 – Fundamentals of Immigration and Naturalization Law.

- Fundamentals of Immigration and Naturalization Law;
- Immigration and Nationality Act (INA);
- United Nations Treaties and/or Conventions;
- Enhance Border Security and Visa Reform Act of 2002 (P.L. 107-173);
- Immigration Amendments of 1965; the Refugee Act of 1980; the Immigration Reform and Control Act of 1986; the Immigration Act of 1990; and the Illegal Immigration Reform and Immigrant Responsibility Act of 1996;
- Aliens, Immigrants and Non-immigrants;
- "non-citizen;" "legal aliens;"
- "legal permanent residents" (LPRs);

- H-2A for agricultural workers; F-1 for foreign students; J-1 for cultural exchange visitors;

- naturalization process;

- Immigration "Preference" Categories and Numerical Limits;

- 2001 Immigrant Admissions by Category [Chart];

- Nicaraguan and Central American Relief Act of 1997;

- The Naturalization Process;

- Social Security (FICA); unemployment (FUTA);

- Exclusions and Removal (Deportation) from the United States;

- The 9 INA "Grounds of Inadmissibility" to the United States [List];

- DHS Bureau of Customs and Border Protection;

- "Public Charges" Affidavit;

- The Illegal Immigration Reform and Immigrant Responsibility Act of 1996 (IIRIRA);

- The USA Patriot Act of 2001 (P.L. 107-77);

Chapter 16 – What is an "Illegal Alien," exactly?

- What is an "illegal alien," exactly?;

- "In America, no human being is 'illegal';"

- United States "national;" "alien;"

- Alien and Sedition Acts of 1798;

- "unauthorized aliens;" Entered Without Inspection (EWI); "undocumented aliens;"

- Bureau of Citizenship and Immigration Services (BCIS);

- Immigration and Naturalization Service (INS);

- Eligibility for Federal Benefits; P.L. 104-193; P.L. 105-33 and P.L. 105-185;

- Supplemental Security Income (SSI); Medicaid;

- Temporary Assistance for Needy Families (TANF);

Chapter 17 – A Summary of Immigration Law in the United States.

- A Summary of Immigration Law in the United States;

- U.S. Congress; Presidential power;

- 1980 Cuban (Mariel) Boatlift Crisis;

- Haitian Refugee Crisis of 1980s and 1990s;

- Federal immigration law;

- "Naturalized" citizens;

- Federal law 28 U.S.C. § 1251; 28 U.S.C. § 994;

- Federal Sentencing Guidelines;

– immigrant visa and non-immigrant visa;

– History of American Immigration Law;

– "Naturalization Act of 1790;" "free white persons;"

– "free white persons" of "good moral character;"

– 1795 Congressional Amendment of the Naturalization Act of 1790;

– 5-year residency requirement for naturalized citizenship;

– July 9, 1868 Ratification of the 14th Amendment to the United States Constitution;

– In 1870 Congress broadened the process of "naturalization" to permit African-Americans the right to become naturalized citizens;

– Xenophobia (fear and hatred of strangers or foreigners, or anything that is strange of foreign);

– Chinese Exclusion Act of 1882; U.S. President Chester A. Arthur;

– 1921 Emergency Quota Act (Emergency Immigration Act); the Johnson Quota Act;

– Immigration Act of 1924 (Johnson-Reed Act);

– National Origins Act; Asian Exclusion Act;

– U.S. Census figures for 1890;

- 1917 Immigration Act;

- Immigration and Nationality Act of 1952;

- "Modern immigration law;"

- Immigration Act of 1917 ("Asiatic Barred Zone Act"); passed by Congress eventually on February 4, 1917;

- President Woodrow Wilson vetoed on December 14, 1916;

- President Grover Cleveland in 1891;

- President William Taft in 1913;

- President Woodrow Wilson in 1917;

- 1917 Immigration Act;

- 1924 Immigration Act;

- Immigration and Nationality Act of 1952 (INA), also known as "The McCarran-Walter Act of 1952;"

- The Immigration Act of 1917 is actually the forerunner of the INA of 1952;

- Homeland Security Act of 2002;

- U.S. Department of Homeland Security, opened on March 1, 2003;

- U.S. Department of Justice and the Attorney General of the United States;

- Immigration Reform and Control Act of 1986, also known as the "Simpson-Mazzoli

Act," signed by President Ronald Reagan on November 6, 1986;

- Immigration Marriage Fraud Amendments of 1986 (Public Law 99-639), passed into law by Congress on November 10, 1986;

- Immigration Act of 1990;

- Lottery Program;

- Naturalization Act of 1906;

- Visa Waiver Pilot Program;

- U.S. Border Patrol;

- Secretary of Health and Human Services;

- AIDS

- Illegal Immigration Reform and Immigrant Responsibility Act (IIRIRA) of 1996, ("Ira-Ira");

- Immigration and Naturalization Service (INS) vs. St. Cyr, Case No. 00-767, 533 U.S. 289 (2001), 229 F.3d 406, affirmed;

Chapter 18 – American Immigration in the "post - 9/11/2001" Environment.

- American Immigration in the "Post -9/11/2001" Environment;

- "People who love sausage and respect the law should never watch either one being made." – "Attorney's Note," page 2, Understanding The Law: A Primer, by Attorney Charles

Jerome Ware; www.amazon.com (Books), November 2008;

- Bush Administration;

- The controversial "USA Patriot Act of 2001;"

- The "Homeland Security Act of 2002;"

- Immigration and Naturalization Service (INS), which had been in existence technically since June 22, 1870 (for at least 133 years);

- INS superseded the previous immigration agency, Immigration and Customs Enforcement;

- Department of Homeland Security (DHS); Bureau of Citizenship and Immigration Services (BCIS) of DHS; United States Citizenship and Immigration Services (USCIS); U.S. Customs; Federal Protective Service; Federal Air Marshal Service; U.S. Immigration and Customs Enforcement (ICE); U.S. Customs and Border Protection Agency (CBP);

- Section 1010 of Title 1 of the Homeland Security Act of 2002, "Mission" of DHS;

- The USA Patriot Act (2001);

Chapter 19 – The USA Patriot Act of 2001.

- The USA Patriot Act of 2001; P.L. 107-56, 115 Stat. 272;

- Osama Bin Laden;

- President George Bush (#43)
- Attorney General John Ashcroft;
- Department of Justice Audit
- Federal Bureau of Investigation (FBI);
- U.S. District Court Order re FBI;
- Summit, New Jersey and the Homeless;
- Dismissal of the seven (7) U.S. Attorneys;
- The USA Patriot Act Improvement and Reauthorization Act of 2005;
- Investigation of Potential Drug Dealers under the USA Patriot Act;
- "National Security Letters;"
- Public Libraries and the U.SA Patriot Act;
- Other examples of Patriot Act Abuse;
- Internet Service Providers;
- U.S. Biological Weapons Anti-Terrorism Act;
- U.S. Immigration and the USA Patriot Act;
- USCIS; EOIR

Chapter 20 – American Immigration and The USA Patriot Act of 2001.

- American Immigration and The USA Patriot Act of 2001;
- Canada; Mexico;

- Border Patrol and Protection;

- USCIS

- Integrated Automated Fingerprint Identification System (IAFIS);

- President Bush (#43)

- IIRIRA of 1996 ("Ira-Ira") [P.L. 104-208];

- Integrated Entry and Exit Data System Task Force;

- "Machine readable passports;" biometric scanners;

- Detention and Removal of Aliens;

- Immigration Act of 1990 (P.L. 101-649);

- 1993 World Trade Center bombing;

- Immigration and Nationality Act (INA);

- Antiterrorism and Effective Death Penalty Act (P.L. 104-132);

- Violent Crime Control Act of 1994 (P.L. 103-322);

- "S.1424" (P.O. 107-45), September 2001; S Visa;

- Enhanced Border Security and Visa Entry Reform Act of 2002 (P.L. 107-173), or "EBSVERA;"

- Intelligence Reform and Terrorism Prevention Act (P.L. 108-458, or IRTPA;

- the REAL ID Act of 2005, President Bush (#43);

- Emergency Supplemental Appropriation Act for Defense, the Global Ware on Terror, and Tsunami Relief, 2005;

- Consolidated Appropriations Act, 2008, P.L. 110-116;

Chapter 21- Current Immigration Issues in the United States.

- Current Immigration Issues in the United States;

- The Agenda – "Immigration" – The White House; President Barack Obama; 44th President of the United States;

- Current Immigration History;

- Five Periods of American immigration history;

- The "post – 9/11/2001" period;

- Periods of American Immigration history [List]:

(1) the Colonial Period (mid-1500s to mid-1800s);

(2) the mid-nineteenth century (mid-1800s);

(3) the turn of the 20th century;

(4) the post-1965 to September 11, 2001; and

(5) the post-September 11, 2001;

- Current immigrants to the United States settle primarily in twelve (12) states: California, New York, Florida, Texas, New Jersey, Illinois, Georgia, Massachusetts, Arizona, Virginia, Maryland and Washington;

- Current top ten (10) countries from which immigrants come into the United States: Mexico, China, India, Philippines, Vietnam, El Salvador, Cuba, Former USSR, Korea and Dominican Republic;

- "Undocumented," or "Unauthorized," or so-called "Illegal" Immigration;

- Latin American countries; Central America; Asia; Europe; Canada;

- Listing of the distribution of "Unauthorized Immigrants," by State, in the United States as of 2006: California, Texas, Florida, Illinois, New York, Arizona, Georgia, New Jersey, North Carolina, Washington and other states;

- Current Public Opinion and Current Controversy Regarding "Unauthorized Immigration;" Supporters argue; Opponents argue;

Chapter 22- Fifteen (15) Tips for Winning Immigration Cases.

- Fifteen (15) Tips for Winning Immigration Cases

167

1. Preparation.

2. Immigration assistance.

3. Proper filing.

4. Legal assistance.

5. Professional background.

6. Follow instructions.

7. Precision, correctness, timeliness.

8. Proper address delivery.

9. Timing.

10. Priority dates.

11. Receipt confirmation.

12. Document originals versus copies.

13. Response.

14. Follow-up.

15. Summary bottom-line check list.

Good-Luck!